P9-CAO-104

COMFORT IN THE CRUISING YACHT

Also by Ian Nicolson

Log of the *Maken*
Sea Saint
Building the *St Mary*
Small steel craft
Surveying small craft
Outboard boats and engines
Dinghy cruising
Designers' notebook
Marinize your boat
Yacht designers' sketch-book
Build your own boat
Improve your boat
Guide to boat buying
Cold moulded and strip planked wood boatbuilding
Boat Data Book
The Ian Nicolson Omnibus

Comfort in the Cruising Yacht

by Ian Nicolson

SHERIDAN HOUSE

To Alasdair Reynolds

In memory of the sea trials of *Longa* (12 feet overall)
January 21st 1984. Gareloch
Wind: Force 6 and rising
Sea state: Rough and getting worse
Land conditions: Deep snow, drifting

In the text SL refers to Simpson Lawrence
of 218 Edmiston Drive, Glasgow G51, Scotland.

Copyright © Ian Nicolson 1987

All rights reserved. No part of this publication may
be reproduced or transmitted, in any form or by any
means, without permission.

First published in the United States of
America 1987 by Sheridan House Inc.,
145 Palisade St., Dobbs Ferry, N.Y. 10522

ISBN 0–911378–68–5

Printed in England

Contents

Introduction

Two of us, both young naval architects, went off for a cruise in a twelve-footer. She was an entirely open boat, without even a short foredeck. Her clinker planking was aged and beginning to soften. Her sails were that grey colour which tells of years of hard work, strong winds and long days of sunshine . . . all the things which make sails old and tired.

She was a pretty boat with a sweeping sheer and an old-fashioned rounded bow. We loved her dearly and would have taken her across oceans if only we had had the time. Instead, we were away for the weekend, and as dusk fell on the first night, the wind dropped completely. The calm was so perfect that the water seemed to have a glossy skin on it. We felt we could have walked to the nearby shore, across the sea's surface.

Using the last of the ebb tide, we drifted out of the main channel and stowed the limp sails when we reached the shallows. Not even a small yacht, creeping along the shore to cheat the tide, would sail so far from the channel. There were only inches below the keel when we lowered the little anchor and started brewing up coffee by the last of the fading light.

Squatting on the bottom boards, I was leaning over the single-burner primus stove, stirring the coffee and sugar into the hot milk and water. It is at moments like this that we all know why we go cruising. The silence was sharpened by the distant cry of a single curlew. Down channel we saw the stern light of the overnight ferry which was working up speed as she reached the open sea.

I was just about to lift the pan off the stove when the wash from the ferry hit us. We were lying beam on to it. There was a brief warning as the breaking crest splashed nearby, glinting in the dusk's dim light. The next moment the boat gave a jolting roll. Too late, I grabbed the pan and cooker. There was milk, made sticky with coffee and sugar, all over the bottom boards. Mixed with it was paraffin from the primus. Some of this wet mess went on the sleeping bags we had been getting ready. The rest of it trickled through the slots in the bottom boards. We mopped up most of the mess and started brewing again.

The boat had a small persistent leak, even when moored, so we sponged her dry before going to sleep.

The first grey light of dawn was seeping through the mist when I woke. On the edge of the tide the feeding seabirds could be heard chattering. During the night the bilge water had risen above the bottom boards so I was lying with my cheek in a puddle of seawater, coffee and paraffin.

Forty minutes later we had bailed and mopped the boat dry, cleaned up, cooked breakfast and got under way, using the dawn breeze to take us towards the open sea. There was no other sail in sight and the bliss was total.

Thirty years later my wife and I were guests on a yacht so large that her smallest boat was well over twelve feet long. We had a cabin as big as a bedroom in a city apartment. Three times a day the talented chef produced meals which were so good we wondered if we could lure this fellow out of his galley and back to our home. Of course, we knew it was a day-dream as we could have not afforded his wages for a month.

Each evening the captain, whose pay was even higher than the chef's, mixed a special brew of rum and cream and fruits and heaven knows what else, so that all activity on the ship stopped, and conversation also ceased while the first few reverent sips were savoured. Soon the rum would begin to make itself felt and the conversations would restart, slowly at first, then building to a cheerful crescendo which only hesitated when we went below to the dining saloon for another of those memorable meals.

These two wildly contrasting yachts were both comfortable, according to their owners. Comfort is not a measureable quality, mainly because it means different things to different people. It also changes according to the weather, the time of year, the size of the boat, the distance from land, the prevalence of seasickness, and the state of the drinks locker.

I've been on a boat in conditions so cold that we could not get the calor gas to crawl out of the cylinders and down the pipes to light the stove. We had to hug the cylinders to transfer our body warmth, and make the gas vapourize and flow down the pipes. At the time I remember being surprised that I did not think things were unduly tough because I had my children with me and they were enjoying themselves so much, no one could carp at any slight inconvenience. But then children in their early teens have an unlimited capacity for boisterous enthusiasm which eliminates thoughts of discomfort.

Most people agree that the worst discomfort offshore is seasickness. The way to beat this plague is to find a pill which is effective but has no side effects, and take it in plenty of time before setting out. The drug has to be helped. It's no use dining on curry and champagne followed by sour, green apples, and expecting the pill to overcome such foods. It is best to stay on deck, but it is madness to forget to put on oilskins until the boat is out of harbour and the spray is already whipping across the deck. People prone to seasickness should make up a bunk before setting out on a voyage, even a short one, and either stay on deck or dive quickly into the bunk. It pays to undress lying down.

The diet should be of dry biscuits. Even after being sick, it is best to eat a biscuit or two. You wait perhaps twenty minutes, maybe only ten, and then start nibbling biscuits. It is important to keep the stomach supplied with something to be sick with, even if the biscuits have little chance of imparting any nutritional goodness, before they return to daylight.

Introduction

Next to seasickness, most people hate the cold more than anything. Cold comes most often by getting wet, so a comfortable boat is one which keeps her crew dry on deck and below. This book has a lot of ideas on this subject, and if some aspects of the matter seem to be missed, then the author's other books should be read. Having sailed in leaky boats and creaky boats, in boats with no noticeable freeboard and with hatches like colanders, I know the discomforts of being wet. Once a boat is afloat it is not so easy to stop leaks through the deck, at port holes, chain-plates and tank filler caps. In the shelter of a boat-shed, or at least under a stout tarpaulin, it is not difficult to frustrate potential leaks through cockpit locker lids and fore hatches. So comfort starts with good fitting out.

Once afloat, a lot of extra comfort can be harvested by being clever. When going down a channel, whether it is ten miles wide or a hundred yards wide, it usually pays to stick close to the windward side. Here the seas will be lower, and if any sort of trouble occurs with gear or propulsion, there is sea room to leeward to give you time to reorganize.

In tidal areas, when working to windward in severe weather, the tide can often be used to ease the boat gently along towards her destination, almost hove to. Certainly progress will be slow, but it will be far more comfortable than thrashing hard into the wind. Having the engine just ticking over helps too.

Where the wind is not directly down a channel, hugging the windward side and short tacking can make the journey fun and reasonably fast, whereas out in mid-channel it will be bumpy, possibly dangerous, and highly disconcerting.

Comfort does not have awkward limitations. It does not need professional skills to make the most of the gear and gadgets shown in these pages. And even if some help is required, perhaps from a sailmaker or boatyard, for the fabrication of a part, very often you can save money by doing the fitting yourself.

Whatever is being made or altered, it pays to use the best materials, the finest fastenings, the most reliable finishing and the best components. The cost of excellent wood is little more than shoddy rubbish, and good materials often pay for themselves in time saved in making the fitting. In future years, a gadget made from good materials goes on working well long after the poorly constructed one has to be replaced. When at sea in rough conditions, if the whole crew know that everything on board is of the best, they will have peace of mind, which is the greatest comfort of all.

Ian Nicolson
Cove, 1986

ALL WITHIN ARM'S REACH OF THE NAVIGATOR

Once settled in his seat, the navigator wants all his equipment close to hand. He does not even want to have to go across to the galley and grab a bar of chocolate, if conditions are hectic.

The layout shown here includes such conveniences as a special shelf for the next chart to be used, and a stowage slot for the charts when they have been used. This means that it is seldom necessary to lift the chart table top to rummage through the main locker for an urgently needed chart.

The front of the book shelf is painted with that special matt black paint used on blackboards so that important information can be chalked up and quickly changed. This can be more convenient than pinning up pencilled notes.

When designing anything like a chart table it is well worth finding out what size of standard drawer is available so that the furniture can be planned round these. This is a great way to save money and time.

POUCH BEHIND BACKREST FOR SPARE SWEATER ETC.

POCKETS FOR SPARE PENCILS SEWN TO CUSHION SIDE

NAVIGATOR'S OILSKINS STOWED BEHIND FOLD-DOWN PANEL

STOWAGE SLOT FOR NEXT CHART NEEDED

BLACK-BOARD ON DEEP BOOKSHELF FIDDLE

TIDE LIGHTS   START TIME

CHART LOCKER

Ian Nicolson

DRAWERS ALL STANDARD DEPTH WIDTH & LENGTH

POUCH FOR LOG-BOOK

POUCH FOR FLASHLIGHT

POUCH FOR TIDE-TABLES ETC.

STOWAGE SLOT WITH FIDDLE FOR CHARTS JUST USED

TILTING CHART TABLE & STOOL

If a yacht is pounding along on one tack for a long time, much of the discomfort of navigating can be eliminated by having a chart table which is pivoted so that it can be roughly level. If there is an attached stool for the navigator he can beaver away, well wedged in place, and all the while his paraphernalia will not slide off the chart table.

A strong base is needed to take the weight of the table and the navigator, so a set of stainless steel tubes bolted to the hull structure is called for, or a pair of bulkheads. The table is pivoted with a locking arrangement to prevent the navigator's weight from causing an upset. It is an added luxury if the electronic instruments can tilt with the table, as shown here.

All sorts of stools can be used, but the type made from a length of tube with a tractor or motor-cycle (or for small craft, a bicycle) seat clamped on is easy to assemble. The navigator splays his feet well apart and there must be tread strips to prevent him slipping.

T-BAR LINKS INSTRUMENT CASING TO CHART TABLE SO BOTH TILT TOGETHER

NAVIGATION INSTRUMENTS IN CASING

LOOSE CABLE ALLOWS FOR CASING MOVEMENT

SUPPORT PILLAR WITH BOLTED FLANGES AT TOP AND BOTTOM

PIVOT BOLT SUPPORTS BRACKET PLATE

CHART TABLE AND CHART STOWAGE

SUPPORT TUBE

BRACKET PLATE BOLTED TO TABLE

PIN THRO' HOLES IN QUADRANT & BR'K'T PLATE

TREAD STRIPS

1½ INCH ~ 40MM BORE TUBE WITH FLANGED END BOLTED TO TABLE

MOTOR-BIKE SEAT CLAMPED ONTO TUBE

NOTE PILLAR, BRACKET PLATE, QUADRANT AND PIVOT BOLT ETC. ARE REPEATED AT OTHER END OF CHART TABLE

SEAT FRONT TO BACKREST FRONT
15 INCHES ~ 375 MM

SEAT TOP TO UNDER SIDE
OF BACKREST BETWEEN
4 & 10 INCHES ~ 100 & 250 M

SEAT ANGLE 95° TO 110°

SEAT TOP TO TABLE
EDGE 11 INCHES ~ 275 M

BACKREST HEIGHT
8 INCHES ~ 200 M

1 INCH ~ 25 M

SLOPE 1 IN 5.

SEAT TILT 3°
BUT VARIABLE

FOOTREST

TABLE
HEIGHT
30 INCHES
760 MM

LOCKING BOLT

Ian Nicolson

SEAT SLIDES

SEAT
WIDTH
14 TO 16 INCHES
355 TO 405 MM

6 INCHES
150 MM

2 INCHES ~ 50 MM

FOOTREST RANGE

SEAT HEIGHT 16
TO 21 INCHES ~
405 TO 535 MM

SLIDE FORW? 4 INCHES ~ 100 M

SLIDE AFT 8 INCHES ~ 200 MM

IDEAL DIMENSIONS OF CHART TABLE & NAVIGATOR'S SEAT

For maximum comfort, a chair must accommodate different sizes of people by being variable. The height of the back-rest, the distance from the seat front to the table front, and other critical dimensions have to be chanegd from person to person.

Almost as important, after anyone has been sitting in one position for a long time, relief from aches can be found by changing the tilt of the seat, sliding it back or forward, raising or lowering the foot-rest, and so on.

The chair and table shown here are based on researches done by V Burandt and E Grandjean, but modified to suit conditions in a boat. The basic seat may be a standard office chair mounted on a base, in turn set on a pair of standard seat slides as fitted in a car (but protected from corroding) or a pair of sail track lengths. The locking bolt holds the chair in place and can be an ordinary barrel bolt, or better still, a pair, one on each side.

AN UNOBTRUSIVE CHART TABLE

The beauty of this design of chart table is that it folds into a small space when not needed, but it is not portable and is effortlessly flipped down into its in-use position in a second. Tables which are unlatched and lugged half way across the cabin, then dropped into tricky sockets are a menance because once at sea no one can set them up.

The table is in two halves which will normally be the same size, though this is not absolutely essential. The outer edge of the outer part is hinged to a shelf front, and the two halves are also hinged together. Some owners, especially those who are, shall we say, just a little clumsy, will want a batch of barrel bolts or turn-buttons to hold the table in the down position.

The ledges on which the table rests when down are L-shaped so that the table never scratches the bulkheads when being lowered.

A favourite material for the chart table is $\frac{1}{2}$in (12mm) marine ply, but the next size down can be used provided everyone is careful, and provided the inboard edge stiffener is tough. It might be 2in × 2in (50mm × 50mm) in section, glued and screwed at 5in (125mm) intervals.

Ian Nicolson

SHELVES AND INSTRUMENTS — PARTIAL BULKHEAD

LEDGES EACH SIDE

SETTEE

CHART TABLE FOLDED DOWN   B   B

HINGE LINE

FIDDLE STIFFENS CHART TABLE EDGE

A

EDGE OF CHART TABLE

½ INCH 12 MM

⅝ INCH 15 MM

¾ INCH 20 MM

SECTION AT B-B
ENLARGED DETAIL

BARREL BOLT AT EACH END SECURES FOLDED CHART TABLE

SHELVES AND INSTRUMENTS

TABLE IN FOLDED POSITION SHOWN DOTᴰ

SECTᴺ AT A-A

HINGES

PARTIAL BULKHEAD

CHART TABLE BEING FOLDED

WOOD LEDGE [SEE DETAIL]

STITCHING EACH SIDE OF BATTEN

TWO LAYERS OF TRANSLUCENT CLOTH

WOOD OR FIBREGLASS BATTEN WITH ROUNDED EDGES AND ENDS

ENLARGED DETAIL

MAIN HATCH OVER CABIN STEPS

SPRAY-PROOF CURTAIN PULLED ACROSS AND TIED TO BULKHEAD EDGE

CURTAIN STOWED

LASHINGS ROUND CURTAIN

NAVIGATOR'S SEAT

BULKHEAD

CHART TABLE

PLAN VIEW

KEEPING THE NAVIGATOR DRY

In rough conditions the navigator squats on his seat at the foot of the companionway steps, trying to work out where the yacht is. Many of the electric gadgets are dead through too much moisture, taken internally. The larger waves tumble along the deck and swoosh through the main hatch, onto the navigator and all his gear. The charts become wetter than sodden toilet paper, and the navigation books soggy, with many of their pages stuck together.

To avoid this chaotic situation, a simple waterproof curtain is needed. In good weather it can be kept rolled aft, behind the navigator's seat, or rolled upwards and secured above by the hatch edge. If the latter stowage is used, the curtain will drop downwards, and may need velcro along the sole to hold the bottom.

The curtain in the sketch unrolls and is pulled forward to the bulkhead edge where a few ties hold it in place. It can even double as a leeboard, holding the now dry and cosy navigator in his seat.

To keep the curtain from bellying, it may be necessary to have battens sewn in, as shown in the detail at the top. These battens will certainly help when stowing the curtain.

The Navigation Area

KEEPING THE CHART DRY

When the navigator goes below to work on the chart in damp conditions, his oilskins drip all over the place, and water seeps or sploshes in through the hatch.

To keep the chart dry this ¹/₄in (6mm) clear plastic cover is ideal. At the top it has one of those plastic watertight hinges; down each side it has a well-bedded fiddle which prevents water oozing round each side; and water which collects on top drips off the bottom edge.

Ideally, the chart – which is shown dotted – is well inside the four edges of the top cover. If necessary, the chart should be folded so that it is ¹in (25mm) in from all four edges.

Chart work is done with that type of felt-tip pen which is easily, but not too easily, wiped off after use. The chart must be clipped immovably with drawing table springs, otherwise the marks on the cover will not be over the correct points on the chart.

COVER & CHART TABLE BOTH HINGE UP
BOTH NEED CLIPS OR PROPS TO KEEP THEM UP

WATER-TIGHT HINGE
FLUSH HINGE
HARD-WOOD FIDDLE
PERSPEX COVER
CHART
CHART TABLE
STOWED CHARTS

SECTION THROUGH CHART TABLE

PERSPEX OR SIMILAR TRANSPARENT COVER
FIDDLE
CONCEALED SCREWS
DRIP THROWER
CHART IN USE
CHART TABLE

SECTⁿ AT 'A-A ENLARGED DETAIL

FELT TIP PENS ARE USED ON TRANSPARENT COVER FOR CHART WORK

BULKHEAD
WATER-TIGHT HINGE
SPRAY THROUGH MAIN HATCH

INSTRUMENTS BEHIND PERSPEX SCREEN

B

PERSPEX FRONT PULLED OUT

SIDE CURTAIN

Ian Nicolson

VIEW AT **A-A**

CHART TABLE

NAVIGATOR'S VIEW OF CHART TABLE

VIEW AT B

INSTRUMENT

PERSPEX FRONT FIXED TO WOOD SIDES AND TOP

BULKHEAD

P.V.C. SIDE CURTAINS ALLOW PERSPEX FRONT TO BE PULLED FORWARD SO THAT INSTRUMENTS CAN BE REACHED

ENLARGED DETAIL SECTION AT C-C

SPRAY DEFLECTOR OVER THE NAVIGATION INSTRUMENTS

In very bad weather, water comes through the main hatch and splashes onto the chart table, wetting everything around. Instruments which are not waterproof suffer expensive damage. They need a cover which allows them to be used, yet protects them from waves coming aboard.

This shield consists of a perspex front with wood top and sides. The top extends back to the bulkhead where there is a hinge which may be a broad strip of pvc material, or something similar. Secured down each side of the perspex there are broad curtains of pvc or some other waterproof cloth. These curtains are wide enough to allow the perspex front to be pulled away from the instruments when the navigator wants to reach up under the cover and twiddle their knobs.

To keep the shield pulled forward there may be locking friction hatch props, or 'skylight openers', such as the Simpson Lawrence patterns 1908601, or 1908604 or the bar type quadrant stay, SL pattern 1908802. These are all fittings which hold hinged covers at different angles.

CHART TABLE EDGES

The chart is indicated by the dotted line. The navigator wants an arrangement whereby his chart edge is kept flat and pinned down, yet is easy to change even in rough conditions. Section 1 has the virtue that the chart can be seen through the perspex, but the parallel rulers cannot operate against the clear material. Section 2 is in some ways better as the parallel rulers can be used right down to the edge of the board, and any length of chart can be fed down through the slot.

Among the virtues of Section 3 are simplicity and strength. In addition, the upstanding part of the wood edging does act as a fiddle, so if the table tilts, pencils will not roll off.

If the ends of the slot are closed there should be drain-holes at each end otherwise in wet weather a puddle will accumulate under the lip.

Strength and stiffness are also virtues of Section 4, but as the navigator leans over the chart-board he may chafe the chart, or wet it.

CHART [SHOWN DOTTED] SLIDES UNDER PERSPEX

PERSPEX BETWEEN 2 & 4 INCHES ~ 50 & 100 mm WIDE

PERSPEX ABOUT ¼ INCH ~ 6 mm THICK

①

GLUED REBATED EDGING

CHART PASSED THROUGH SLOT

SLOT BETWEEN ¼ & ½ INCH 6 & 12 MM

NAVIGATOR LEANING ON BOARD EDGE DOES NOT DAMAGE CHART

②

ALL EDGES WELL ROUNDED

CHART HELD DOWN BY WOOD LIP

BUILT-UP SECTION STRENGTHENS CHART TABLE A LOT

③

NO REBATING NEEDED

EPOXY GLUE IN ALL JOINTS

Ian Nicolson

EDGE RADII AT LEAST ⅜ INCH ~ 10 MM

④

CHART FOLDED ROUND AND TUCKED BETWEEN WOOD BATTEN AND BOARD

WOOD BATTEN BETWⁿ 2½ & 5 INCHES ~ 60 & 125mm BY ABOUT ½ INCH ~ 12 MM

SECTIONS THROUGH INNER EDGE OF CHART TABLE

BOTTOM RIGHT HAND
CORNER OF CHART TABLE

VIEW AT **A**

DRAWER PULLED OUT

MILES
COURSE
WEATHER

CHART TABLE
CHART LOCKER

SHOCK CORD
LOG BOOK OPEN

A

B

Ian Nicolson.

EVEN WHEN DRAWER IS OPEN
AMPLE LENGTH REMAINS IN SLOT

DRAWER PULLED OPEN
FOR WRITING UP LOG

LOG-BOOK ALWAYS READY FOR USE

PENCIL BOX

SHOCK-CORD HOLDS
BOOK OPEN

DRAWER SIDE

DRAWER HAS NO FRONT

ENLARGED DETAIL
VIEW AT **B**

LOG BOOK STOWAGE

Unless it has a special stowage space, the log book is likely to become an orphan, or be shoved in among other books, or left sliding about on the chart table, or, perhaps, jammed in a netting rack beside the navigator's perch.

A good stowage place is a special drawer which pulls out from under the chart table. This drawer has no front, so that the log book can be written up in its stowage place. To hold the book firmly as well as open at the right place, there are two strips of shockcord fixed to the bottom of the drawer at the correct distance apart to hold the pages down. These shockcords can also hold a piece of polythene sheet over the book to make doubly sure that it stays dry.

If this drawer is on the far right of the chart table it can be opened without the navigator having to move, but it will only suit a right-handed person. It could pay to have a drawer on each side of the chart table, and use the second for the nautical almanac or the tide tables.

A PENCIL (& EVERYTHING ELSE) HOLDER

The usual type of pencil holder positioned over chart tables the world over has an upper and lower shelf. The top shelf has a row of holes drilled in it, each hole slightly larger than the diameter of a pencil. Only pencils fit through these holes, but navigators and the rest of the crew need a 'universal' holder which keeps all sorts of other things safe and ready to hand.

This 'universal' holder has two thick strips of that squashy foam plastic used inside modern cushions, with a gap of about $^1/_8$in (1mm) between the two strips. All sorts of small gadgets can be pushed down between the twin cushions and they will still be there after sailing through a gale.

The length of this holder can be as long as the chart table is wide, but in practice this will mean that everything from the bread knife to the skipper's false teeth will end up there. So it is probably best to make this rack about 10in (250mm) long.

BACK PIECE OF 'UNIVERSAL' PENCIL HOLDER

PLASTIC CUSHION MATERIAL GLUED TO WOOD FIDDLE

PLASTIC CUSHION MATERIAL GLUED TO BACK PIECE

PLAN VIEW

BULKHEAD

WOOD FIDDLE

BIROS AND OTHER PENS

CHART PENCILS

DECK FILLER CAP KEY

PENCIL STUBS

'PENCIL' FLASHLIGHT

DIVIDERS

ELEVATION

Ian Nicolson

2 INCHES 50 MM

1½ INCHES 40 MM

BOTTOM SHELF AT LEAST ⅜ INCH ~ 10 M THICK

PERSPEX FIDDLE 1 INCH ~ 25 M HIGH HOLDS RUBBERS SPARE BATTERIES SELLOTAPE ETC.

BULKHEAD BY CHART
TABLE OR FURNITURE FRONT

GAPS BETW'N PEGS 9½ INCHES
~240 M FOR A4 SIZE PAPER
WHICH IS 8¼ INCHES~210 M WIDE

BASE BLOCK MATCHES
BULKHD OR FURNITURE

ROW OF WOOD
CLOTHES PEGS

Ian Nicholson

PEGS MAY BE PAINTED
DIFFERENT COLOURS

ELEVATION

CORNERS AND EDGES WELL ROUNDED

BOTTOM ROW OF PEGS PREVENT PAPERS
WAVING ABOUT BUT ARE NOT ESSENTIAL

SECTION

PEGS MAY BE EPOXY GLUED IN
PLACE WITH OR WITHOT SCREWS

NAVIGATOR'S NOTICEBOARD

It is so handy to have a display area over the chart table, where important information can be arrayed. Tide times for the weekend, a reminder to replenish the gas bottles, train times for getting home. These are the sorts of information we need near at hand.

However, not everyone likes having drawing pins on a boat. They rust, and they fall on the sole, sharp point upwards, which is no fun for bare-foot crew.

A clothes peg (or clothes pin as some people prefer to say) board has lots of advantages. It does away with drawing pins, and the pegs can be colour-coded so that important information is held up by the brightest red pegs, and less important items by duller pegs. Each peg can hold several sheets of paper, or even things like the class racing flag, a spare pencil, or cash for the harbour master's dues.

A single row of pegs suits most boats, but some people prefer an upper and lower row, so as to retain the top and bottom edges of each piece of paper.

WARM PLATES & GIMBALLED COOKERS

A meal is so much better if the plates are warmed, and this can be done painlessly if the plate storage shelf is made of stainless steel and is located above the cooker. There should be large holes in the shelf, and it must be small enough to keep the plates from slamming about when the boat rolls.

The gimballing of cookers is an art. For a start, the pivot level must be high but not too high, and the ballast, in the form of the stove and the pans on it, must be heavy but not too heavy. Experimentation is the best way to find the right location for the pivot and the correct weight. In general, the pivot should be high, say level with the middle of the pans unless there is an oven, in which case it can be one third of the way up the deepest pan. Weight can always be added to the bottom of a cooker to make it more stable.

Standard cooker fiddles are nearly always too low; they should be at least 3in (75mm) high even if they have to have cut-outs for the pan handles.

IT MAY BE HARD TO REACH THIS SHELF ONCE THE COOKER IS LIT

FIDDLE HEIGHT MUST SUIT HEIGHT OF PLATE PILE

GIMBAL PIVOT AT HALF PAN HEIGHT

PLATES STOWED IN STAINLESS STEEL RACK WARM UP WHEN COOKER IS LIT

PANS NEED CLAMPS AS WELL AS FIDDLES

FIDDLE 3 INCHES ~ 75 MM OR MORE ABOVE TOP OF COOKER GRID

SWINGING SPACE FOR COOKER MUST CATER FOR A 90° KNOCK-DOWN

VERY LITTLE HEAT FROM STOVE GETS INTO THIS LOCKER

WHEN COOKER IS LIT THIS LOCKER IS INACCESSIBLE

IF GIMBALLED COOKER IS UNSTABLE WEIGHT IS ADDED TO THE BOTTOM

EACH GIMBAL BRACKET NEEDS FOUR RELIABLE 3/16 INCH ~ 5MM BOLTS

Ian Nicolson

SEC$\text{T}^{\underline{N}}$ THROUGH FRIDGE

STAINLESS STEEL MESH RACKS

SUMP WITH DRAIN PLUG

SPRAY UNIT PRESSURISED

PRESSURISED HOT & COLD FRESH WATER SYSTEM

SALT WATER PUMP

FLUSH LID ON DEEP LOCKER FOR 3 BOTTLES

STAINLESS STEEL PILLAR

PERFORATED CUP FOR DRAING CUTLERY

DEEP NARROW SINK HOLDS DIRTY DISHES

SINK

2 FEET ~ 600 $\overset{M}{M}$

COOLG UNIT IN RECESSED FRIDGE

SECONDARY SINK 6 INCHES ~ 150 $\overset{M}{M}$ WIDE

Ian Nicolson.

"PUT-DOWN" SPACE

DOOR TO AFT DOUBLE CABIN

UP TO COCKPIT

PLAN VIEW OF THE 'FEELING 1040' GALLEY

The cook works safely in the confines of the C-shaped galley; in bad weather there is little chance of being thrown far. On the right of the sink is the saltwater pump, so it is the one most likely to be used as most people are right-handed, and this tends to save water!

The secondary sink on the right can be used to hold dirty dishes until there is time to wash them, or, after washing, they can be left to drain in this mini-sink which is narrow but also deep and safe. Ahead of it is a deep locker for stowing three large bottles. The deck-head support, in the form of the stainless steel pillar, is oval in section so as to take up the minimum space athwartships.

In the fridge there are two shelves, each with fiddles, set in such a way that the top one is narrower than the lower one, to give a view of the food stowed on the 'lower deck'. The sump makes it easy to dry out the fridge after defrosting, and washing out is helped by the presence of a proper drain complete with plug.

TWIN SINKS & THEIR SURROUNDS

Sinks should not be fitted hard up against a bulkhead otherwise the person washing up lacks elbow room. If the space between sink and bulkhead is quite small, and it needs to be no more than 6in (150mm), it is too narrow for putting down plates. But it can be made into a trough-type draining board. This consists of a watertight recessed box made of metal, wood or fibreglass, into which wet cups, plates and cutlery can be put.

That narrow space beyond the sinks is ideal for another trough, less deep, and designed to hold standard plastic or glass containers for foods like salt, sugar, tea and so on. This trough should be designed so that the containers drop in easily.

The wood covers on the sinks form cutting boards; they have one corner cut away to take the drips from the pumps, and to allow them to be easily lifted off. One board is cut to take mugs when they are being filled.

PLAN VIEW OF TWIN SINKS

FOOT OPERATED EMERGENCY FRESH WATER PUMP,

ELECTRIC POWERED HOT & COLD SUPPLY,

SALT WATER PUMP

FRONT OF UPPER L'K'RS

STORAGE BOXES FIT IN DEEP TROUGH LOOSELY

SALT

FRESH

O

HOLES FOR HOLD⁹ MUGS

CUTAWAY IN WOOD COVER ON SINK

TROUGH WITH DRAIN FORMS DRAINING BOARD AND OPEN-TOPPED STOWAGE

PARTIAL BULKHEAD

DISTANCE MAY BE AS LITTLE AS 6 INCHES ~ 150MM

SECTION

LOOKING AFT

EXTRA HIGH FIDDLE

PAINT TIN OR SIMILAR

CLAMPS

FIDDLE BEING LAMINATED

"KICK SPACE"

ROUND CORNERS REDUCE BRUISES

FIDDLE 4 × 5/8 INS. ~ 100×15 M

SCREWED DOWN CHOCKS

BUILDING BASE

ENLARGED DETAIL

ORIGINAL SIZE OF PUT-DOWN SPACE

NEW PUT-DOWN SPACE EXTENDS OVER SETTEE

SETTEE

PLAN VIEW

HIGH LAMINATED FIDDLE ROUND ENLARGED WORK-TOP

MORE WORKING SPACE FOR THE COOK

To give the cook more 'put-down' space, just make up a big tray and screw it down on top of the existing working surface. The tray is made larger than the existing work top by extending it inboard, forward, and possibly aft. The forward overlap steals a little space over the settee, but does not stop three or four people sitting there. The inboard extension is acceptable because when people stand close to a work surface they need more room at sole level than at work top level.

The neatest way to make the new tray is to laminate the fiddle, and for seagoing use this should be good and high. The enlarged detail shows how to bend the laminates round a curved tin to get lovely corners. It is usual to have a hard-wearing plastic laminate on the work top surface but some people prefer to use an epoxy resin paint or varnish.

Galleys

GIMBALS FOR A BIG COOKER

A set of gimbals made to this design carries the weight of a heavy cooker. The parts can be made away from the cooker because sizes do not have to be accurate to the nearest $1/4$in (6mm) provided the base width is slightly greater than the cooker width.

The side straps bend easily in at the top and middle to hug the cooker, and the fastenings through them can be located wherever it suits. The channel bars are drilled with rows of holes so that the pivot height can be varied. Typically, the channels will be 8in (200mm) from top to bottom. The bottom flat bars under the cooker will be separated by a distance of about three quarters the athwartships dimension of the cooker, unless they simply must be set under the cooker feet.

A barrel bolt or other locking device is essential to stop the cooker swinging when the gimballing effect is not needed.

ENLARGED DETAIL VIEW AT Z

GALVANISED OR STAILESS STEEL FLAT BARS 1×⅛INCH ~25×3MM
BOLTS THROUGH COOKER BOTTOM
BOTTOM FLAT BARS SUPPORT THE COOKER

SEE ENLARGED DETAIL X ON NEXT PAGE

SIDE FLAT BAR BENDS IN AGAINST COOKER SIDE

SEE ENLARGED DETAIL ABOVE Z

PIVOT BAR
CHANNEL BAR SUPPORTS PIVOT
TWO BOLTS EACH SIDE THRO' FLAT BAR & COOKER

FRONT VIEW OF COOKER

BARREL BOLT STOPS COOKER SWINGING ON PIVOTS IN HARBOUR OR DURING A CALM
WOOD CHOCK FOR BARREL BOLT PLUNGER END

BOLT THROUGH COOKER SIDE

Ian Nicolson

FLAT BARS 1×⅛ INCH ~ 25×3MM

SIDE OF COOKER

ANGLE BAR 1×1×⅛ INCHES 25×25×3MM

ENLARGED DETAIL ~ ALTERNATIVE VIEW AT Z. SEE OPPOSITE PAGE

A

VIEW AT A-A

COOKER FOOT BOLTED TO ANGLE-BAR

SEMI-SOFT WASHER

DOUBLER

GALLEY SIDE

CHANNEL BAR

PIVOT BAR 3/16 INCH 8MM DIAMETER

B

BOLT LOCKS COOKER IN PLACE

BOLT SUPPORTS PIVOT BAR

PIVOT BAR

RUBBER

PLAN VIEW

LOCK NUT

DOUBLY ENLARGED DETL AT X ON PREVIOUS PAGE

VIEW AT B

GIMBAL DETAILS

At the top is a sketch showing an alternative way of supporting the cooker. Instead of horizontal flat bars, a pair of angle bars take the weight of the cooker. They fit under the cooker feet with bolts through the feet.

The bottom two sketches are doubly enlarged to show the details of the pivoting. The pivot bars have triangular brackets under, (as shown on the front view of the cooker on the opposite page) and the rest on rubber blocks. These dampen the swing. If the boat inverts, the locking bolts above the pivots prevent the cooker romping away from the galley and terrorising the crew.

There must be three bolts through each channel bar of about $3/16$in (5mm) diameter, and they need not be countersunk provided they are clear of the pivot bars.

GIMBALLED WORKING SURFACE

When far out at sea and slaving over the stove, there is nothing so handy for the cook as a level surface for putting down cups and plates. When soup has to be taken off the stove and poured into mugs, the job is so much easier, and if a stew has to be spooned into plates, life is less fraught if the plates are on a gimballed surface.

This design makes use of the gimballed cooker to which it is attached. Three pivot points are needed and they must be exactly in line. All the ballast is provided by the cooker, so it may be necessary to bolt a steel plate to the bottom, to counteract the weight of a fully laden pan resting on the high gimballed put-down space.

High fiddles are essential at sea because plates and mugs can slide, even on a gimballed surface.

GALLEY WORK-BENCH TOP

FLANGED BRACKET BOLTED TO GIMBALLED PUT-DOWN SPACE

PUT-DOWN SPACE GIMBALLED WITH COOKER

FIDDLES ROUND PUT-DOWN SPACE 3 INCHES ~ 75M HIGH

BRACKET BOLTED TO COOKER AND TO GIMBALLED PUT-DOWN SPACE

GIMBALLED COOKER

SMALL BULKHEAD

PUT-DOWN SPACE

COOKER MAY NEED BALLAST

ALL THREE PIVOTS MUST BE EXACTLY IN LINE

3×¾INCH~ 75×20mm SUPPORTS EACH SIDE SWING UP TO HOLD
TABLE HORIZONTAL~FORMING AN EXTENSION TO THE GALLEY

TABLE ANGLED DOWN ABOUT 10° FOR
COMFORTABLE CHART WORK

TABLE HORIZONTAL FOR USE BY COOK

FLUSH HINGES

Ian Nielsen

PENCIL SHELF WITH LOW FIDDLE
ABOVE LEVEL OF STOWED CHARTS

HOLE IN PLY BASE 2 OR 3 INCHES~50 OR 75 M DIAMᵗᵉ
FOR DUSTING OUT LOCKER & PUSHING CHARTS UP

SECTION THROUGH CHART TABLE & LOCKER

CONVERTING THE CHART TABLE FOR GALLEY USE

Few galleys have enough working space, and many cooks end up with plates and cups on the cabin sole. It so happens that on many boats the chart table is opposite the galley, and in harbour the chart table is seldom in use. So, if it can be used by the cook, so much the better.

A sloping chart table is easily levelled with simple but strong turn-buttons, one at each side. A single turn-button is not a good idea because at times the cook may use the chart table for cutting up tough meat, or slicing through hard cheese, and then the load will be heavy.

Some details in the sketch concern the navigator. So that the charts lie absolutely flat on the table, the hinges should be the flush type, with no part standing up from the smooth surface. The best place for the pencil shelf is high at the back because this uses space otherwise wasted. That hole in the chart locker bottom is a real asset not only when dusting out, but also for pushing up a heavy heap of charts so as to retrieve one buried in the pile.

MUG RACK FOR ALL WEATHERS

If a yacht is slamming into a head sea, or rolling horribly in a swell, the crew will find a simple rack for mugs, near the cooker, a real boon. This rack will suit a variety of galleys, and can be easily made by amateur or professional. The ideal material is a wood which matches the rest of the trim round the galley.

The rack can be fixed permanently, or, as in the sketch, made portable. It will normally be in place all the time the boat is at sea, and the cook can fill the mugs without taking them from the rack. A similar rack could be made to take deep soup bowls.

If the top of the partial bulkhead is horizontal, and the top moulding is shallow, the rack will tend to tip sideways, at least slightly, so it will be necessary to glue chocks to the bulkhead to fit the 'skirts'. These chocks will thicken the bulkhead locally and ensure that the inside faces of the 'skirts' are held rigidly.

WIDTH TYPICALLY 4 INCHES~ 100 MM TO SUIT ALL SORTS OF MUGS

FIDDLE DEPTH TYPICALLY 2½ INCHES~ 60MM TO SUIT A VARIETY OF MUGS

ENLARGED SECTION THROUGH MUG-RACK

BULKHEAD TOP MOULDING

PARTIAL BULKHEAD

"SKIRTS" ON MUG RACK

SIX MUGS IN PORTABLE RACK

WOOD PILLAR

CHOCK BETW'N "SKIRTS"

GALLEY WORK-TOP

Ian Nicolson.

MOULDING ON TOP OF PARTIAL BULKHEAD

OUTBOARD

ELEVATION

HAND PUMP FOR SALT
OR FRESH WATER

SINK

SECTION VIEW

LARGE DRAWER CLOSE
UNDER SINK

LOCK WITH ACCESS
TO SEA-COCK

SINK DRAIN-PIPE
AND TRAP

SEA-COCK

SIDE COMPARTMENTS ARE
IDEAL FOR LONG KNIVES ETC.

PLAN VIEW

SINK DRAIN

WATER
PIPES

MIDDLE COMPARTMENT CAN
HOLD SMALL TOOLS OR JAM JARS

THICK DRAWER ENDS

LIGHT THIN SIDES

MARINE PLY BASE

A DRAWER BENEATH THE SINK

Because sinks have to have drains, the space beneath the sink bowl is often wasted. However, a clever joiner can make up a special drawer, shaped like a thick U, to slide under the sink and yet avoid all the piping.

The base of the drawer should be of marine ply, probably about $^3/_8$in (10mm) thick, to give the drawer ample rigidity. The ends will be of hardwood, typically $^3/_4$in (20mm) thick, but the sides can be lighter. If the whole drawer is assembled and glued up with epoxy resin, it will gain the stiffness it needs to cope with its odd shape.

Anyone who has a drawer, or indeed any bit of furniture, which is becoming floppy because it is an unusual shape, can stiffen it by gluing in fillets at the corners.

FRYING PAN LOCKER

A frying pan takes up a lot of space, and because of its shape, it is not easy to stow in such a way that it 'stays where it is put'. This special locker uses up what is sometimes a wasted space beside the cooker, or maybe between the sink and the edge of the galley bench.

The special locker is narrow, and just high enough to accept the pan through the slot in the front. The pan drops down inside the locker and jams automatically between the locker front and the soft foam plastic cushioning at the back. This cushion may be covered with leather cloth or a similar washable material.

To clean out the locker, remove the pan, turn the top and bottom turn-buttons and remove the front panel. Ideally, the inside should be lined with a smooth, washable plastic material like that used on galley bench tops.

SLOT IN LOCKER FRONT IS JUST LARGER THAN PAN DIAMETER ~ SAY X PLUS 2 INCHES ~ 50 MM

TURN-BUTTON

SECTION AT 'A-A' SLIGHTLY ENLARGED

TURN-BUTTON

SOFT PAD HOLDS PAN

COOKER

PAN DIAMETER 'X' INCHES OR MILLIMETRES

TURN-BUTTONS TOP AND BOTTOM

PAN GOING INTO LOCKER

FRONT PANEL OF LOCKER IS PORTABLE FOR EASY INTERNAL CLEANING

ELEVATION OF GALLEY

VIEW OF LOCKER FRONT WITH PAN WEDGED IN PLACE

VIEWS AT 'A' ~ ALTERNATIVE FORMS OF CONSTRUCTION

END STOPS ON TUBES

SLIDING COLLAR

BACKREST AT LEAST 8×3 INCHES~ 200×75 MM

VARIABLE HEIGHT TUBE

CLAMPS

AT LEAST 15 INCHES~375 M M AND MAYBE FULL LENGTH OF GALLEY

METAL EYES EACH SIDE FOR ENDS OF GALLEY STRAP

PIVOTING WOOD BACKREST MAY BE PADDED OR CURVED

A

HOOP OF STAINLESS STEEL OR GALVANⁱˢᵉᵈ STEEL TUBE

B

Ian Nicolson.

GALLEY STOVE OR SINK ETC.

BASE~PLATE SAME MATERIAL AS TUBING SIZE ABOUT 8×4×¼ INCH~200×100×6MM

FOUR BOLTS 5/16 INCH~8 M M DIAMETER

ENLARGED DETAIL AT 'B'

COOK'S COMFORT

A strong pipe, bent like an out-size croquet hoop and bolted to the sole in the galley, makes a great prop for the cook. On one tack the cook leans against the hoop, and on the other the 'galley strap' is hooked onto each side of the hoop to hold the cook off the stove. For extra comfort there is a wooden pad for the cook to lean on, and this can have fiddles to hold the cook in place if the boat is pitching a lot. These fiddles are not shown in the drawing, but are at each end of the pad.

The hoop may be made to fit one person, as shown top left, or the crossbar can be varied up and down, to suit a range of heights as detailed top right. The hoop may extend the full length of the galley, and could even have two pads though not every cook likes an assistant working alongside.

The base of each vertical tube must be strongly bolted, never screwed, to the cabin sole, with suitable doublers to take the shock loadings of people lurching against the bars.

DEALING WITH RUBBISH

Call it a 'gash bin' or a 'trash bucket' or a 'rubbish box' or a 'garbage container'. Call it what you like. It holds all the waste material thrown out by the cook during the preparation of a meal. This design fits the available space under the galley work top even if the boat slopes in sharply, or it can be squeezed into the corner of an engine bay, or under a cooker . . . in short, it can be worked into all sorts of odd-shaped spaces.

The basic box will probably be made of $1/2$in (12mm) marine ply, or on a racing boat out of $1/8$in (3mm) marine ply with lightening holes and stiffeners. It will not become particularly dirty as it is lined with the same sort of plastic bags which are sold for kitchen use. To prevent the bin swinging open when the boat heels, there is a simple pivoted bar, made from a length of brass about $8 \times 3/4 \times 1/8$in ($200 \times 20 \times 3$mm). This locking device can be used on other types of stowage, and the whole bin concept can be used for keeping things other than kitchen waste.

SECTION AT 'B-B'

PIVOT BOLT

B BAR TILTS

LOCKED NUT

PIVOTING BAR KEEPS RUBBISH BIN CLOSED

Ian Nicolson

B

SLOT FOR HAND

FRONT OF RUBBISH BIN

ENLARGED DETAIL AT 'A'

BIN IS OPENED BY PUSHING PIVOTING BAR ASIDE AND PULLING FRONT INBOARD

A

RUBBISH BIN FRONT IN OPEN POSITION

BIN SHAPED TO FIT SPACE INSIDE HULL

LIGHT ROPE CHECKS AMOUNT BIN TIPS OUT

REPLACEABLE PLASTIC BIN LINER FOLDED OVER AT TOP

TWO STRONG HINGES

VENT AND DRAIN HOLES 2inch 50MM DIAMETER ROUND BOTTOM

GALLEY WORK-BENCH — STAINLESS STEEL LIFT-UP HANDLE SIMPSON LAWRENCE No 1919901 OR −902

LIFT-OFF LID

ENLARGED DETAIL AT Z−Z

GALLEY RUBBISH DROPS INTO BIN OR BUCKET

B — 4½ INCHES ~ 115 MM

PLAN VIEW

TO SUIT STANDARD PLASTIC BAGS 2×A+2×B IS LESS THAN 46 INCHES ~ 1.170 METRES

A

5½ INCHES ~ 140 MM

GALLEY WORK-BENCH — LID LIFTS OFF

RUBBISH BIN LOCKER

DIMENSION C MUST BE LESS THAN 27 INCHES ~ 675 M TO ALLOW BAG TO BE FOLDED OVER AT TOP

C

PLASTIC BAG TOTAL LENGTH IS 30 INCHES ~ 750 MM

ELEVATION

Ian Nicolson

MORE RUBBISH

When cooking, it is amazing how much rubbish is produced. There are potato peelings, empty tins, plastic wrappings and much more. All this has to be put into a container with the minimum fuss and inconvenience. A very good arrangement is shown here. It consists of a bin or bucket located below the galley work top, with a hole in the work top through which all the rubbish is pushed. The hole is covered by a simple lid which has a 'lift-up' handle let into it.

The hole in the work top is made just big enough to take a large tin or jam jar. A larger aperture would be obtrusive. The container below the hole can be a bucket or plastic bin or a specially-made box of wood, metal of fibreglass. Its size should suit the standard plastic bag designed for domestic rubbish bins, that is, about 27in (675mm) deep, and the perimeter of the top rim must be a little under 46in (1200mm) so that the plastic bag can be folded over it.

A GALLEY STRAP

The bottom drawing shows the type of comfortable galley strap which is made from a length of Terylene webbing and a broad pad of sailcloth sewn to the middle of the belt. This wide backrest prevents the webbing from digging into the cook's back, and sometimes has pockets for a cooking knife, or cloth or tin opener.

The middle two sketches show a standard adjustable buckle which makes it easy for the cook to alter the length of the belt with one hand. There must be four $^3/_{16}$in (5mm) bolts through the base-plate of the buckle and the same number through the eyeplate which takes the snap-hook on the other end of the belt. Those light alloy carbine hooks favoured by climbers make good clips for the belt end.

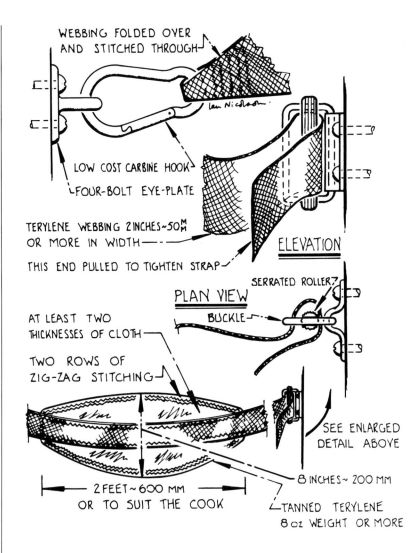

WEBBING FOLDED OVER AND STITCHED THROUGH

Ian Nicholson

LOW COST CARBINE HOOK

FOUR-BOLT EYE-PLATE

TERYLENE WEBBING 2 INCHES ~ 50 ^M_M OR MORE IN WIDTH

THIS END PULLED TO TIGHTEN STRAP

ELEVATION

PLAN VIEW

SERRATED ROLLER

BUCKLE

AT LEAST TWO THICKNESSES OF CLOTH

TWO ROWS OF ZIG-ZAG STITCHING

SEE ENLARGED DETAIL ABOVE

2 FEET ~ 600 MM OR TO SUIT THE COOK

8 INCHES ~ 200 MM

TANNED TERYLENE 8 oz WEIGHT OR MORE

GALLEY STRAP OF TERYLENE OR
CANVAS OR P.V.C. CLOTH

ONE HAND OPERATED SNAP
SHACKLE LIKE S.LAWRENCE № 5415001

TRACK SLIDER WITH
LOCKING PLUNGER

VARIABLE LENGTH
LIGHT LINE LASHING

HAND-RAIL

HAND-SLOT
4½ INCHES
110 MM

SOLID SECTN
2 INCHES~
50 MM

TRACK END
STOPS AT
TOP & BOTTOM

SHEET LEAD
TRACK

Ian Nicolson

BULKHEAD

DISH-CLOTH POCKET FOR
LEFT-HANDED PEOPLE

DISH-CLOTH POCKET ABOUT
10×8 INCHES~ 250×200 MM

COOK'S SAFETY STRAP

When working in the galley in rough sea conditions, the cook needs a strap to prevent him, or her, being flung about. As cooks vary in height, some arrangement is needed to make it easy to shift the strap up and down. On the left there is a length of track such as is normally bolted down on deck to take genoa sheet leads. It can be the lightest available track, often 1in (25mm) wide. A standard slider, of the type normally used to take the shackle which holds the sheet lead block, is fitted on the track. A spring-loaded plunger holds the slider at the correct height, and the snap shackle on the safety strap engages in the metal eye on the slider. At the other end, a lashing can be used and this will allow the cook to vary the tension of the strap.

On the right there is a vertical handrail, with close-spaced slots. These slots must be wide enough for a large man's hand, so this means the 'jump' from one strap location to the next must be 4½in (110mm) which may not suit everyone.

TOAST FOR BREAKFAST

Some cookers have no grills for making toast, and some have grills which make dreadful toast, and some have grills which take hours to make a couple of pieces. This simple gadget makes good toast at a reasonable speed, and as it is not too bulky to stow, there is no reason why the average cruiser should not have one for each top burner on the cooker.

The bread may need moving about slightly to give it that even brown crispness we all so much enjoy, and it will probably be advisable to have a pair of tongs to turn the toast over because every part of this toaster gets hot.

The height from the top of the cooker's burner to the under side of the lowest layer of wire mesh is important, so it will be best to make this about 1in (25mm) at first and gradually shorten it to about 3/4in (20mm) to allow fast toasting with no burning.

ALL RODS FORMING FRAMEWORK ABOUT 1/8 OR 3/16 INCH~ 3 OR 4 OR 5MM DIAMETER

ALL ROD ENDS FULLY WELDED

ANY SIZE PIECE OF BREAD CAN BE TOASTED BUT MAY NEED MOVING ABOUT

ELEVATION

ALL FOUR SIDES LOOK LIKE THIS

ABOUT 1¼ INCHES~30MM

TOP OF COOKER

Ian Nicolson.

THREE LAYERS OF STAINLESS STEEL WIRE MESH

CALOR BURNER

ABOUT 3/4 INCH~20 MM. ADJUST AFTER EXPERIMENTS

MESH WIRE ABOUT 1/16 INCH ~ 1·5MM THICK

PLAN VIEW

ABOUT 5 INCHES ~125 MM BUT MADE TO SUIT COOKER

GAPS IN MESH ABOUT 1/8 INCH~ 3 MM

ABOUT 5 INCHES ~125 MM BUT MADE TO SUIT COOKER

TEAK COVER FORMS "CUTTING BOARD"

BEVELLED EDGE FOR EASY LIFTING UP

5/8 INCH 16 MM

ENLARGED DETAIL OF LID TOP

WORKBENCH TO SURFACE

1/4 INCH ~ 6MM GAP ALL ROUND FOR EASY FITTING

2 INCH ~ 50MM OVERLAP

OUTSIDE FILLET MAKES IT EASY TO FIT INSULATION

INSULATION BLOCKS DROPPED IN PLACE

PIPE TO PUMP

COOLING UNIT

6 INCH ~ 150MM HIGH FIDDLE FOR BOTTLES

SUMP WITH GRATING OVER

PLASTIC DRAIN PIPE

TANK COLLECTS MELTED ICE

ICE-BOX OR FRIDGE

This design for an ice-box can be used for making a fridge, if a bought-in cooling unit is used. Though mass-produced fridges are cheap, they are not always easy to install. They seldom make the best use of available space; they are rectangular which does not suit the average boat; and they are seldom really well insulated.

This drawing shows a good type of fridge or ice-box with a simple type of lid which does not have to be fitted accurately. It is a bonus that this lid doubles as a chopping board for cooking.

Melted ice drains into a tank where it can be pumped off, a better practice than the more usual arrangement whereby the water drains into the bilge. Though this fridge or ice-box is shown under the galley bench, it can be situated under a side-board or even under a chart table provided the navigator is able to sit adjacent in comfort.

ICE-BOX DESIGN

By using a 'stepped section' for the interior of this ice-box, extra space is gained. The top shelf can be used for a cooling unit run off a battery, turning the ice-box into a fridge.

The interior casing is made of fibreglass or ply lined with fibreglass. It is carefully placed in position, and the gaps between it and the hull, the bottom plinth, and the side walls are filled with foam polymer which is poured in. Before pouring the foam the drain is fitted, and all likely leak holes where the polymer might escape are sealed off.

Most cooks like a smooth, uninterrupted work top so the cold-box lid is made flush fitting, with recessed hinges and lifting ring. The lid is bound to be at least slightly bulky and heavy so it is not a good idea to omit the catch which holds the lid, or make the lid portable. If the lid is not a tight fit, heat will seep in and reduce the effectiveness of the cold-box.

FLUSH FITTING LID WITH FLUSH HINGES

DEPTH LIMITED TO ABOUT 1 FT 8 INCHES ~ 500 MM AND REACH ACROSS COUNTER TO UNDER 12 INCHES ~ 300 MM

LID LIFTING RING FITS FLUSH

BOTTOM SLIGHTLY SLOPED TO HELP DRAINAGE

MINIMUM INSULATION THICKNESS 3 INCHES ~ 75 MM BUT 5 INCHES ~ 125 MM MUCH PREFERRED

LOCKERS & DRAWERS FORM EXTRA INSULATⁿ

Ian Nicolson

LID CATCH MUST BE STRONG

LOCKERS

FIDDLE

POURED-IN INSULATION

HULL FORMS PART OF INSULATION

LIGHT PLY OR FIBREGLASS

STANDARD SKIN FITTING FOR DRAIN

DRAIN PIPE TO SPECIAL TANK OR BILGE

MARINE PLY WORK-TOP┐ BOLTS ┐ ┌─HINGE RECESSED AND STONGLY FASTENED

┌─WOOD DOUBLER

└POLYURETHANE OR P.V.C. GLASSED ON BEFORE TOP IS FITTED

BOTTOM SLOPED AND RECESSED FOR DRAINAGE┐

┌MARINE PLY LINED WITH FIBREGLASS

┌CORNERS GLUED AND SCREWED

Ian Nicholson

└NUT AND FLANGE WELL BEDDED

STAINLESS STEEL HOSE CLAMP┘

└POLYURETHANE OR P.V.C. INSULATION GLASSED ON

ICE-BOX DETAILS

Only marine grade plywood should be used when making an ice-box, because there is plenty of moisture about, and lesser grades of wood will rot and disintegrate too soon. The thicker the ply, the better the insulation as wood is remarkably good at keeping the heat out.

The drain fitting is a plastic skin fitting sold in chandlery shops. The type with a thin flange is best if good drainage is required. One leaf of the lid hinge is shown bolted through, and the other held with long screws into a doubler which extends round the opening. To make the glassing in of the ice-box straightforward, the heaviest cloth used should be $1\frac{1}{2}$oz chopped strand mat, and even then all exterior edges should be well rounded, while interior corners will need filleting. The fillets can double as joining strips for the sides, top and bottom, but both glue and screws are needed at all wood joins.

A BUILT-IN ICE-BOX OR FRIDGE

To make a container for keeping food and drinks cold, a well insulated box is needed. This can be made of ply, with blocks of insulating material secured to the outside by simple glassing-on techniques. The sides of the box in this sketch reach well below the bottom to take extended side insulation.

A plinth is made to support the ice-box, and the box itself is designed to make the best use of available space. Before the box has been lined with fibreglass it is lowered in behind the galley front, and the galley work top (which has been previously assembled with its insulation) is fixed down. The interior of the ice-box is now glassed in, though in practice one or two layers of the glass may have been applied before fitting the top.

For the drain pipe only plastic materials are used because metal will act as a conductor and reduce the effectiveness of the insulation.

INSULATED WORK-TOP FITTED AFTER ICE-BOX HAS BEEN BUILT IN AND PLUMBED

INSIDE CORNERS FILLETED TO AVOID SHARP INTERIOR ANGLES WHEN FIBREGLASSING

ACCESS HOLE TYPICALLY 12 × 12 INCHES ~ 300 × 300 MM FOR EASY CLEANING, FILLING, ETC.

EASILY WASHED SMOOTH FIBREGLASS INTERNAL LINING

POLYURETHANE OR P.V.C. GLASSED ONTO PLY OR FIBREGLASS

AVOID METAL DRAIN-PIPES TO MINIMISE HEAT LOSS

STRONG PLY BASE WITH STIFFENERS SUPPORTS ICE-BOX

MINIMUM DRAIN PIPE BORE ½ INCH ~ 12 MM TO AVOID BLOCKAGES

ACCESS TO PIPE JOIN IN LOCKER UNDER ICE-BOX

Ian Nicdea

SETTEE TOP

1¼ INCH ~ 30MM 10 GAUGE COUNTERSUNK SCREWS AT 6 INCH ~ 50 MM CENTRES

FLANGE AND CASING SIDES ETC TYPICALLY ⅛ INCH ~ 3MM THICK

1 INCH ~ 25 MM

LID AT LEAST 3INCHES 75MM THICK

WOOD DOUBLER

1½ INCHES 40 MM

WELL ROUNDED EDGE

AT LEAST 3INCHES ~ 75 MM

FOAM FILL

ENLARGED DETAIL

SETTEE CUSHION

SETTEE FRONT

FIDDLE

SEE ENLARGED DETAIL ABOVE

ALLOW A GAP OF AT LEAST ¾ INCH ~ 20 MM FOR DRAINAGE ETC.

DRAIN HOLE AT END

Ian Nicolson

AN UNDER SETTEE ICE-BOX OR FRIDGE

A long, fairly shallow ice-box can be fitted under a settee, provided the crew do not mind the inconvenience of lifting the cushion to get at the food. The cushion improves the insulation, as does the dead air space round the box. By making the box long, it can either have a very good capacity, or one end can hold the refrigerating unit, if the old-fashioned ice-box is not acceptable. Electrically driven cooling units can be bought from chandlers and bolted in place inside the insulated container.

The handle for lifting out the lid must be recessed, and the surface flange all round must be made quite thin otherwise the cushion will not lie flat on the settee base. Where the flange meets the box there has to be a full-rounded fillet for strength. So that the fibreglass does not chip, the lid and box edges are made with soft radii, as shown in the sketch.

When cleaning, painting or repairing the hull, the top flange screws are removed and the whole casing is lifted out.

A LOW PRICE ICE-BOX

The quickest and cheapest way to fit an ice-box in any boat is to buy one of those portable boxes sold by shops catering for campers and caravanners. These boxes are available in a variety of sizes and shapes, though most are longish, and have about the same height as width.

Because a ice-box is obtrusive in most cabins the first thing to do is to investigate a suitable stowage places, and measure up each one. Then a selection of different boxes are measured in shops to see which will fit. There must be room to lift the box in place, and space at the sides for at least two lashings. The crew will want to get at the food without moving a lot of furniture and certainly without moving the box from its stowage space.

Shown here are some of the possible places where an ice-box might be stowed. If the worst comes to the worst, it can be banished to a cockpit locker, or to the fo'c'sle, but these are less convenient places than near the galley.

CABIN ENTRANCE

TWO LASHINGS OF ¼INCH~6 MM DIAMETER TERYLENE OR SIMILAR

COOL BOX IN SPECIALLY BUILT CASING OVER SETTEE END

FOOT OF SETTEE GOES UNDER COOL BOX CASING

BERTH BASE PANEL LIFTS OUT FOR ACCESS TO BOX

TWO LASHINGS ONTO EYE-PLATES EACH END

COOL BOX BELOW SETTEE IN CUT-OUT RECESS IN SOLE

GLASSED-IN PLY BASE BELOW SOLE LEVEL

COOL BOX UNDER STEPS HELD BY TWIN LASHINGS

STEPS MAY NEED MODIFYING TO MAKE ROOM FOR BOX

FIDDLES TYPICALLY 4×⅝ INCHES~100×16MM HOLD COOL BOX

Ian Nicolson

GLASSED-IN NUT

BOLTS AT 3 INCH
75 MM CENTRES

SEMI-SOFT BEDDING
2 INCHES~50 MM WIDE

COCKPIT SIDE

GLASSED-IN WOOD

ALTERNATIVE TECHNIQUES

ENLARGED DETAIL

AT 'A-A'

SEMI-PORTABLE PANEL

HINGED LIDS NEED SWINGING
ROOM TO OPEN

SMALL HATCH

SEMI-PORTABLE
PANEL

COCKPIT
WELL

A

A

Ian Nicolson

TWO GLASSED-IN VERTICAL
PLY SUPPORTS ½ INCH~12 MM THICK

SIDE FIDDLES ALMOST UP TO LID LEVEL
ENSURES COOL BOX ALWAYS STAYS IN PLACE

COOL-BOX STOWAGE

A bulky cool-box may not fit in a cabin and that odd-shaped space inside the counter could be just the place for it. If the access hatch in the deck is too small, don't make it bigger: it's much better to saw out a panel at the aft end of the cockpit well, to get the box in place.

It is important that the well side is made truly watertight which explains why the sealing strip is wide, and the fastenings close together. When the panel is out, it will be easy to glass-in the two rests for the box and the high end fiddles which are so important. No one wants lashings over the top of a cool box if they can be avoided as they have to be taken off every time the lid is lifted.

The techniques shown here can be used for stowing other bulky items, such as generators, extra fuel tanks which are piped up, and perhaps extra batteries.

A QUICK, CHEAP ICE-BOX

This sketch shows what must be the quickest way of fitting a boat with an ice-box. A standard mass-produced box which will fit in the aft end of the cockpit is bought and secured in place with a fiddle across the fore end. One or two side fiddles may be needed too, or maybe just a chock of wood between the ice-box and the cockpit well sides will be adequate.

To keep the ice-box in place in all conditions, a heavy cloth cover is bolted down across the fore end of the aft deck, and stretched over the box. A tight lacing or row of thick shockcord loops keeps the cover down. If the cover is white it will not get hot even in bright sunlight, and if it is of double or triple thickness it will not only be extra strong, but it will also provide better insulation. Even if the box is not as wide as the cockpit well the cover should be, so that the sun cannot reach the sides of the ice-box.

FORWARD

THICK CLOTH COVER PROTECTS 'COOL BOX' FROM SUN

TILLER SWEEPS OVER AFT END OF COCKPIT MAKING A DEAD SPACE

A

COCKPIT WELL

FIDDLE

COOL BOX IN DEAD SPACE AT AFT END OF COCKPIT

THICK CLOTH COVER WITH BRASS EYELETS ALONG BOTTOM

LACING TO HOOKS FIXED AT 6 INCH ~ 150 MM CENTRES ON FIDDLE

HARDWOOD FIDDLE 3×¾ INCH ~ 75×20 MM

ENLARGED DETAIL AT "A"

END LASHINGS LED DIAGONALLY OUTWARDS

LASHINGS LED SLIGHTLY OUTBOARD OVER BERTH

ROPES ABOUT ¼ INCH ~ 6MM

RING AND TURNOVER OR HYDRAULICALLY PRESSED EYE

EYE SPLICE

LEE-CLOTH

POCKET FOR CLOTHES ETC.

VIEW AT A

ENDS CUT DIAGNLY FOR VENTILATION

10 OUNCE CLOTH

CUSHION

B

SEAMS DOUBLE-STITCHED

SECTION

LOOKG FORWD OR AFT

VIEW AT B

ALL EDGES TRIPLE THICKNESS

LIGHT LASHING THRO' BERTH BASE

EYELETS AT 5 INCH ~ 125 MM CENTRES

LEE-CLOTHS

Berth leeboards which are made from a cloth material are sometimes referred to as lee-cloths. They may be made from a Terylene (Dacron) cloth available at sailmakers, or an acrylic material, such as is sometimes used for sail covers and cockpit tents. If a dark material is used it will show the dirt less.

Top and bottom securing arrangements must be strong. For instance, those brass eyelets which are hammered in are not strong enough for the upper lashings, so either the traditional 'ring-and-turnover' or the modern equivalent, the hydraulically pressed eye, must be worked in.

It is common practice to screw a wood batten over the edge of a lee-cloth along the bottom, but this makes it a chore to take the cloths out for cleaning, and the 'over-&-over' lacing shown here, through the berth base, has much to commend it.

A LEEBOARD FOR DOUBLE BERTH

A cloth leeboard which extends down the middle of a double berth must be pulled tight down at the bottom. An eyeplate is needed for this beneath the mattress at each end. The thin rope which runs through the bottom seam of the leeboard is passed through each eyeplate, then back up to the tough eyelet at the end of the leeboard. After putting the line through this eyelet it is hauled tight and knotted. This keeps the leeboard well down and prevents it sliding up or down the berth.

Lashings at the top corners are secured to eyeplates on strong points about 4ft (1.2m) above the berth, and ideally there should be a central eyeplate above the middle of the berth to take the extra lashing.

This type of cloth leeboard is considered much more comfortable than a wooden one, especially as the latter tends to be so heavy and awkward to stow if it is high enough for all sea conditions.

BULKHD

SEAM AT BOTTOM OF LEEBOARD

END OF LINE PULLED TIGHT THEN KNOTTED

LINE LEADS TO OTHER END OF BERTH

MATTRESS

ENLARGED DETAIL

EYEPLATE

OPTIONAL EXTRA LASHING UP TO EYEPLATE

LASHINGS ¼ INCH 6 MM DIAMETER

BOLTED EYEPLATE

LASHING

SEE ENLARGED DETAIL

Ian Nicolson.

AS OTHER END

LEEBOARD 16 INCHES ~ 400 MM SHORTER THAN BERTH

LEEBOARD 14 INCHES ~ 350 MM AT LOW POINT. 20 INCHES ~ 500 MM AT HIGH POINTS

MATTRESS

LINE PULLS LEEBOARD TIGHT DOWN ON TOP OF MATTRESS

SECTION AT Z-Z

EDGES WELL ROUNDED

THIS EDGE FLAP ON CUSHION FASTENED FIRST

LEEBOARD CUSHION 2 OR 3 INCHES ~ 50 OR 75 M/M TYPICAL THICKNESS

SCREWS THRO' BOTTOM FLAP

MATTRESS THICKNESS 3, 4, OR 6 INCHES ~ 75, 100, OR 150 MM

WOOD DOUBLER

Ian Nicolson

BERTH BASE

DOUBLER PIECE

ALL EDGES WELL ROUNDED

"BOTTLE-TOP" CAPPING

HAND GRIP AND VENT SLOT

SCREWS CONCEALED

BERTH LEEBOARD OR COAMING

BERTH THIS SIDE

BERTH THIS SIDE

A WOODEN LEEBOARD

The top sketch shows how to make a leeboard less shoulder-bruising by using a cushion. The cushion covering will normally match the mattress covering, but it will have flaps, like flanges, sewn along two edges. The cushion is held up, and the top flap is screwed in place with 8-gauge countersunk screws at 6in (150mm) intervals. Then the cushion is dropped in place and the bottom flap screwed with the same screws at double the above spacing.

The sketch at the bottom left shows a leeboard with a hand-grip slot to make it easier to get into the berth. This slot, or row of slots provides ventilation for the person in the berth if there is a high cloth leeboard. The sketch at the bottom right shows the traditional 'bottle-top' section beloved of good boat builders because it looks superb when well made.

A CABIN GRAB-RAIL

For anyone who cannot do
woodwork up to the standard of the
furniture in his cabin, this grab-rail
is excellent. It also has the merit that
it can be located anywhere under the
cabin top deck, and two or even
three of these ropes can be rigged.
They can be taken down when the
boat is in harbour, if, for instance,
they obstruct the headroom, and
they can be fitted over a galley, up
forward, in a toilet compartment and
so on.

The eyeplates, never eyebolts, at
each end must not be the decorative
type which have little strength, but
the type sold for securing on deck to
take blocks and so on. To get the
rope tight, a dinghy type tackle,
ideally with a built-in cleat or
jammer is used, or if preferred, a
rigging screw can be fitted.

ENLARGED DETAIL

CABIN TOP DECK

DECK FITTING TYPE EYEPLATE

FOUR 3/16 INCH~5MM BOLTS

BULKHEAD

BACK
BLOC

2 INCH~50MM HAND SPACE BETWEEN
CABIN TOP DECK AND ROPE

ROPE TIGHTENED
BY TACKLE

SNAP SHACKLE
EACH END

ROPE 1/2 INCH
12MM DIAMETER

MATCHING CHOCK 5 INS.~ 125 $\overset{M}{M}$ LONG

SCREWS STAGGERED & GEL-COATED OVER

INBOARD

1 INCH~25mm ROUNDED TOP

3 INCH~75mm HARDWOOD GRAB-RAIL MATCHES CABIN FURNITURE

3/4 INCH~20 $\overset{M}{M}$ ROUNDED BOTTOM

JOIN GLUED AND SCREWED WITH 12 GAUGE SCREWS STAG $\overset{RD}{}$

INSIDE OF CABIN COAMING

BOLT HEADS HIDDEN BY GEL-COAT

NUTS HIDDEN FROM VIEW BY FLANGE OF ANGLE-BAR

1 INCH~25 $\overset{M}{M}$ LIGHT ALLOY TUBE WELDED TO 1¼ x 1¼ INCH~ 30x30 $\overset{M}{M}$ ALLOY ANGLE-BAR

SHORT INTERMITTANT WELDS TO AVOID PIPE DISTORTION

Ian Nicolson

3 INCH~75 $\overset{M}{M}$ LENGTHS OF ANGLE-BAR SPACED 12 INCHES~300 $\overset{M}{M}$ WITH EXPOSED EDGE ROUNDED

HANDRAILS INSIDE CABIN TOPS

The upper sketch shows a shapely hardwood handrail, the lower one a metal rail which can be of steel or aluminium alloy, or for someone who wants a boat to be different, polished brass could be used . . . at a high cost. The cabin coamings are shown as being of fibreglass, but they can be of any material. If they are of fibreglass, the fastenings look best if sunk just slightly, then covered over with a carefully matched skin of gel-coat.

These designs have concealed fastenings which always enhance the appearance of any boat. The wooden longitudinal part must be epoxy-glued to the chocks carefully, and the screws must be at least 12-gauge to get a good grip. These screws should penetrate ⅝in (15mm) into the longitudinal rail for the maximum grasp onto that component.

These designs can be used in other locations on board. It is good sense to standardize on items like handrails so that a whole batch for a boat can be made at one time, even though the handrails throughout the boat will be of different lengths.

THERE ARE NEVER ENOUGH HANDRAILS ON BOARD

A shortage of handrails below decks and on deck is the prime cause of bruises and even broken limbs. Handrails on the cabin top backed by similar rails on the underside make a lot of sense. If screws are used to hold the rails, as shown in the top sketch, the rails need to be slightly staggered. This means that the screws in the top rails do not foul those driven upwards from below, yet each set of screws is in the middle of its solid section of rail, between the handgrips.

Bolts are widely considered to be the best fastenings for handrails. They should not be of brass unless they are more than $5/16$in (8mm) diameter, and galvanized steel should be avoided as it tends to rust after a few years unless the end sealing is perfect. Nowadays, stainless steel is the common material.

DOWEL FIXED WITH EPOXY RESIN GLUE
STAGGERED SCREWS
HANDRAIL ON CABIN TOP
1½ INCHES~40mm PENETRATION FOR A SECURE GRIP
CABIN TOP
HANDRAIL IN CABIN

DECORATIVE HEAD SCREWS MUST NOT BE SAND-PAPERED WHEN VARNISHING

DOWEL CLEAR OF ROUNDED EDGES

HANDRAILS ARE FITTED AT RIGHT ANGLES TO CABIN TOPS WITH NO BEVEL ON THE BOTTOM

HANDRAIL WELL CLEAR OF CABIN TO ROUND EDGE

NUT AND WASHER ON TOP
AMPLE BEDDING TOP AND BOTTOM
3 INCHES~75MM OR MORE
CABIN TOP
Ian Nicolson
HANDRAIL IN CABIN

DOWELS AT LEAST ¼ INCH~6MM THICK
BOLTS AT LEAST ¼ INCH~6 MM DIAMETER

METAL TUBE 1 INCH ~ 25 MM
DIAMETER SUPPORTS HANGERS

TUBE IS PERMANENTLY THROUGH
HANGERS WHICH CANNOT FALL OFF

SECTION AT A-A

HARDWOOD CHOCK
BULKHEAD

SLOTS FOR TROUSERS ETC.
1½ INCHES ~ 40MM WIDE
4½ INCHES ~ 110 MM

HOLE FOR TIES
AND BELTS ETC.

ALL EDES
WELL ROUNDED

18¼ INCHES ~ 465 MM

BARS ABOUT 1 INCH ~ 25 MM DEEP

ABOUT 18 INCHES
450 MM

OVERLAP 3 INCHES ~ 75 MM
SECURED BY VELCRO

2 INCHES ~ 50 MM APPROX

METAL PLATE WASHER WITH TWO
COUNTERSUNK 10 GAUGE SCREWS

STRAP TO STOP CLOTHES
SWINGING WHEN BOAT ROLLS

CAR SAFETY STRAP OR **TOE-STRAP** WEBBING

BETTER COAT HANGERS

It is not possible to buy seagoing coat hangers so they have to be made. They have to be 'captive' otherwise they come adrift from their top bar and deposit the clothes in a huddle at the bottom of the clothes locker. This type of hanger, made from $\frac{1}{2}$in (12mm) marine ply or $\frac{3}{4}$in (20mm) solid wood, with well rounded edges, is fitted onto the suspension bar before the latter is fitted into the clothes locker.

The top edges may be padded, and the hole for ties and belts is optional. Some owners will prefer just the single slot for trousers . . . but then, here as elsewhere, when making special fittings for a boat the professional or amateur shipwright can enjoy using his imagination as well as his skills.

SEAGOING DRAWERS

An unbreakable handle on a drawer is all too rare. The one shown here consists of a slot through the front which has a wood doubler over, partly to compensate for lost strength, partly to give a more pleasant grip, partly to improve the look of the drawer front. The size of the slot will accept the biggest, toughest seaman's hand, and it also allows ample air to flow in and out of the drawer to keep the contents dry and sweet-smelling.

To prevent the drawer flying open in a rough sea there is a turn-button, or maybe two, one at each top corner. These can be cut out of hardwood and may have some elegant pattern, perhaps fish or mermaids, carved on the face. It is no good screwing turn-buttons in place, nor are thin, flimsy bolts acceptable.

SECTION AT 'A-A'

HARDWOOD TURN-BUTTON AT LEAST 2½ INCHES~60MM LONG

DOWELLED BOLT AT LEAST 3/16 INCH~5MM DIAMETER

FIDDLE

SELF-LOCKING NUT

Ian Nicolson

SEMI-SOFT WASHER

DRAWER FRONT

FIDDLE

A

A

B

B

TURN-BUTTON TWISTS OVER CORNER OF DRAWER TO PREVENT IT OPENING

FRONT VIEW OF DRAWER

SLOT 5½ × 1¾ INCHES ~ 140×45MM

HAND-HOLE SLOT HELPS VENTILATION

SECTION AT 'B-B'

SCREWS THRO' BACK OF DRAWER

EDGES BEVELLED AND ROUNDED

SWINGING TRIANGULAR METAL PLATE
PREVENTS DRAWER OPENING ACCIDENTALLY

ROUNDED CORNERS

BARREL BOLT

FRONT
VIEW

SECTION

DRAWER
FRONT

TOP PIECE OVER END OF
DRAWER PREVENTS GEAR
FALLING OUT

ROUNDED EDGES
MINIMISE BRUISES

LIMIT STRING PREVENTS
DRAWER COMING OUT TOO FAR

SCREWS PUT INTO HANDLE THIS
WAY NEED NO DOWELS

Ian Nicolson

LONG STRONG PRACTICAL HANDLE

PLAN VIEW

SAFE DRAWERS

It is common practice to make boat drawers with a lip on the bottom, to prevent accidental opening. On modern craft, which are usually light and lively, drawers too often jump up and burst open because the lip is inadequate for holding the drawer shut.

Two techniques are shown here which hold drawers shut with certainty. Top right is the well-tried swinging triangular metal plate. Anyone who wants to add a touch of traditional elegance to a boat can use polished brass, but most people will prefer stainless steel. Top left is the other reliable fitting: a standard barrel bolt which engages in the top flange of the drawer.

To stop the drawer coming right out when pulled hard, a string at the back has much to commend it, being cheap, adjustable and reliable. To prevent gear being thrown out of the back of the drawer when the boat is well heeled there is a cover over the end quarter or one-third of the drawer length.

53

BUNK-SIDE TABLE

The pinnacle of luxury is lying in a snug berth sipping a mug of tea. If there is no bunk-side table, much of the pleasure is lost as the hot mug has to be balanced precariously. And if there is nowhere to put an ashtray and plate of biscuits by the mug, then misery creeps in where there can be bliss.

A portable table which clips onto the berth's wooden leeboard has all sorts of advantages. It can be made quite large, to take a book or two and a transistor radio, but it will not obtrude in a cramped cabin because it can be stowed away when not in use. With luck, the same table can also be used elsewhere in the boat, perhaps on a partial bulkhead in the saloon, or looped over a cockpit coaming.

Construction can be varied to suit available materials and skills. Anyone who is not good at making up wood boxes can use a plastic box as the basis, and stiffen the side which takes the metal hooks with a doubler of wood or metal. Another panel is fixed to the bottom with small bolts to give extra stiffness and that extension which lodges against the leeboard side.

PLAN VIEW

ALL CORNERS WELL ROUNDED

WIDTH SELDOM OVER 10 INCHES ~250 MM BUT MADE TO SUIT OWNER'S NEEDS

LENGTH SELDOM OVER 14 INCHES ~350 MM BUT MADE TO SUIT SPACE ETC. AVAILABLE

AS WIDE AS POSSIBLE

WOOD THICKNESS TYPICALLY ½ INCH ~12 MM

HOOKS MAY ALSO FIT COCKPIT COAMINGS ETC.

PADDING OF CLOTH OR LEATHER ON METAL HOOKS

INSIDE DEPTH ABOUT 2½ INCHES ~60 MM

END ELEVATION

METAL HOOKS ABOUT 1 x 3/16 INCH ~ 25 x 5 MM

BERTH

DEPTH AT CUT-AWAY FOR MUG HANDLE ½ INCH ~12 MM

BASE EXTENSION WITH SOFT PAD RESTS ON BERTH LEE-BOARD

Ian Nicolson.

TELESCOPIC TABLE HOLDER IS ADJUSTED TO SUIT ANGLE OF HEEL

FORK END OF HOLDER LINKED TO BRACKET UNDER TABLE

TABLE TOP IN UPRIGHT OR 'HARBOUR' POSITION

FIDDLE AT LEAST 3 INCHES ~ 75 MM DEEP ALL ROUND TABLE

RIGID SUPPORT AT EACH END OF TABLE

PIVOT

Ian Nicolsd

DOUBLER PAD UNDER SOLE BEARERS FOR TABLE BOLTS

LARGE BRACKET ALLOWS HOLDER TO SWING PORT & ST'BD

DROP-NOSE PIN FIXES TABLE HOLDER AT REQUIRED ANGLE

STABLE TABLE

Gimballed tables have lots of disadvantages. They are costly; they sometimes fail to keep pace with the boat's motion and build up a jerky roll which chucks everything off the table; and they weigh a lot. Worst of all, when gimballing, no one can put a hand on them or they will pivot over and topple the dishes onto a settee.

This tilting table gets over a lot of the above disadvantages. Once the boat has been settled onto a tack the table is pivoted till it is nearly level by pulling the drop-nose pin out of the telescopic holder and putting it back in a new position with the table roughly horizontal. The table has to be designed so that it does not rise too high on the lee side otherwise no one will be able to eat off it, and on the other side it must not close the knee space between the table and the settee.

A SALOON TABLE

If the main framework of a table is made in the form of a box, as shown here, the inside of the box can be used for stowing crockery, cutlery, bottles and so on. Naturally, the box must have a lid, and in this sketch the table top is pierced by two lids which do not extend out to the sides of the box, or to the ends. The lid on the left has deep fiddles secured to one side so that when as shown at the top, the table is flush and suitable for writing or chart work. In the middle sketch the lid has been reversed so that the fiddles stand up, and they are shown cradling two bottles and two glasses.

The right hand lid has a metal cutlery container fixed on the underside. The container need not be this shape, though this one has all sorts of advantages like strength, elegance and reliability, and it can be made of wood, metal or fibreglass.

LIFT-OUT LID HAS FIDDLES ON ONE SIDE. SEE BELOW WHERE FIDDLES ARE UPWARDS

FORE AND AFT

TWO RECESSED LIFTING RINGS IN EACH LID

TABLE TOP

A

A

Ian Nicolson

LOCKER

CONTAINER FOR CUTLERY

SECTN VIEW

SIDE ELEVATION

LIFT-OUT LID TURNED OVER SHOWN HERE KEEPING BOTTLES SAFE

TWO RECESSED LIFT-OUT RING

CONTAINER SCREWED UP TO TABLE TOP LID

CUTLERY CAN BE PUT BACK THROUGH SIDES OR ENDS

SEPARATE COMPARTMENTS FOR KNIVES FORKS AND SPOONS

ENLARGED DETAIL SECTION AT 'A-A'

FRAME-WORK OF 1INCH
25 MM ALUMINIUM TUBE

FRAME-WORK FULLY TRIANGULATED

PIVOT BAR EXTENDS
BETWEEN TWO BULKHEADS

POUCH FOR PENCILS,
LOG-BOOK ETC.

CURVED AND
PADDED BACK-REST

PORTABLE TABLE
WITH HIGH FIDDLES

PADDED ARMRESTS

POUCH FOR FOOD,
FLASHLIGHT, ETC.

LIFE-JACKET
UNDER SEAT

Ian Nicolson.

RUBBER CHOCK PREVENTS SEAT
BANGING HULL AT END OF SWING

FOOT-REST WITH NON-SLIP SURFACE

CLEARANCE NEEDED BETWEEN SWINGING FOOT-REST AND SOLE

A GIMBALLED SEAT

For the single-hander or the ocean cruising crew there is nothing so luxurious, so desirable or so comforting as a safe gimballed seat which can be used in all but the very worst weather.

All sorts of designs can be used, and this drawing shows just some of the features which should be incorporated in a safe, strong and versatile seat.

There must be ample swinging room, but some sort of end stop is needed port and starboard to deal with excessive heel. A lock is essential to keep the seat secure when the gimballing is not required. Since this seat will be used for navigating, reading, eating and so on, a portable table is important. Without a foot rest the seat will not be comfortable, but the rest should be close to the sole.

ALMOST AN ARMCHAIR

On the Hedonist 44 there are a pair of adjacent chairs to this clever design. The most striking feature is the back which is made up of curved tapered strips of hardwood carefully polished. The rest of the chair is of the same material so that quite apart from being a comfortable place to sit down, each seat is a striking piece of furniture.

This sort of seat hardly suits a boat under about 35ft (11m) long, unless she is very much a floating home, but for a deep sea cruiser or a comfortable motorboat it has much to recommend it. The total space it takes up is not large, and it can be positioned by a desk or chart table provided that there is ample room to get in.

Perhaps the principal disadvantage of this form of seat is that it must either face fore-and-aft, or it may be uncomfortable on one tack because the sitter will be tipped out. On the opposite tack it will be bliss.

MOST EDGES ROUNDED TO ¾ INCH ~ 20 MM RADIUS

TOP OF BACK ROUNDED TO 1¼ INCHES ~ 30 MM RADIUS

PLAN VIEW

1 INCH ~ 25 MM

18⅝ INCHES 475 MM

1¾ INS 45 MM

14 INS 355 MM

26 INCHES ~ 660 MM

2¾ INS. 70 MM

A

20½ INCHES ~ 520 MM

3 INCHES 75 MM

19 INCHES 485 MM

5¼ INS. 135 MM

LOCKER

14 INCHES 355 MM

A

SECTION AT A-A

66MM ~ 2⅝ INCHES
20 MM ~ ¾ INCH PARALLEL
20 MM ~ ¾ INCH PARALLEL DOWN TO A
48 MM ~ 1⅞ INCHES
64 MM ~ 2½ INCHES
80 MM ~ 3¼ INCHES
35 MM ~ 1⅜ INCHES
30 MM ~ 1¼ INCHES

20 MM ¾ INCH
40 MM 1⅝ INCHES
50 MM 2 INCHES
40 MM 1⅝ INCHES
75 MM 3 INCHES

A

88 M   78 M   80 M   102 M   135 M
3½   3⅛   3¼   4   5⅜ INCHES

FIRM CUSHIONING
SOFT OR MEDIUM CUSHIONING
75 MM ~ 3 INCHES PARALLEL

50 MM 2 INCHES
58 MM 2¼ INCHES
80 MM 3⅛ INCHES
20 MM ¾ INCHES
55 MM 2⅛ INCHES
59 MM 2¼ INCHES

EACH INTERVAL IS
100 MM ~ 3¹⁵⁄₁₆ INCHES

Ian Nicolson

38   13   22   41   60 MILLIMETRES
1½   ½   ⅞   1⅝   2⅜ INCHES

COMFORTABLE SEATS

These 'offsets' show the shapes of two comfortable seats. They were designed as a result of research work done by V Burandt and E Grandjean, and will fit most people. The top of the backrest should be curved to a radius of 650mm, that is 25½in, and the middle of the backrest curved to a radius of 450mm, which is 17½in.

Both seats have been modified to suit boat conditions, and the bottom one will be the easiest for most people to make as it does not require a contoured seat cushion, just a constant thickness foam rubber cover all over.

These seats can be made from fibreglass, cold-moulded wood, solid wood, or metal. The double curvature of the back is specially designed to give the correct support for the human backbone.

A STOOL FOR GALLEY OR CHART TABLE

A stool which swings to different positions, or swings out of the way when not in use, is ideal for many locations. The top can be made of solid wood without a cushion, or as shown here. The metal-work may be of steel for cheapness, aluminium alloy for lightness, or polished bronze for 'cost-is-no-worry' elegance.

There should be an average height with variations above and below for smaller and larger people. Most people like a seat diameter about 10in (250mm) but some boats are so cramped that an 8in (200mm) diameter may be better. All wood and metal edges are well rounded, and the bracket bolted to the furniture must have six well-spread ¼in (6mm) bolts, with a backing pad behind the support panel.

That split pin, shown on the enlarged detail, centre left, is to stop the seat lifting off accidentally at sea, and the plastic washers under each gudgeon ensure a smooth swinging motion when the seat is pivoted.

ENLARGED DETAILS

¾ INCH ~ 20 MM MARINE PLY

FOUR ¼ INCH ~ 6MM BOLTS

3 INCH ~ 75 MM FOAM PLASTIC CUSHION

COPPER OR BRONZE NAILS

LEATHER-CLOTH COVER

METAL PLATE 5×5×3/16 INCHES ~ 125 × 125 × 5 MM

ROD PINTLE
OUTER TUBE
SPLIT PIN
PLASTIC WASHER

1 INCH ~ 25 MM OUTSIDE DIAMETER SUPPORT TUBE THROUGH PLATE AND WELDED ON TOP

PLATE 5×3/16 INCH ~ 125×5 MM FLANGED TOP AND BOTTOM

SUPPORT ARM OF TUBING

3/16 INCH ~ 5MM BRACKET

STOOL SWINGS

BRACKET BOLTED TO FURNITURE

Ian Nicolson

CUSHION 3 INCHES ~ 75 MM THICK TOP ABOUT 18 INCHES ~ 460 MM ABOVE SOLE

OUTER TUBE HAS HOLES 2 INCHES ~ 50 MM APART TO VARY SEAT HEIGHT

DROP-NOSE PIN OR BOLT THRO' OUTER TUBE

UPPER AND LOWER SUPPORT ARMS

THREE LAYERS OF 3/16 INCH ~ 5MM PLY GLUED TO FORM CURVED SEAT

HOLES IN SEAT MAKE IT "NON-SLIP"

PLY EDGES COVERED BY HARD-WOOD MOULDS

ENLARGED DETAIL

PLAN VIEW

LAMINATED SHAPED SEAT

LEGS 2½ × ⅞ INCH 60 × 22 MM

TIES AS LEGS

Ian Nicolson

ELEVATION

SIDE VIEW

BOTTOM OF LEG

BRONZE SCREW PUT IN THEN HEAD CUT OFF TO FORM PEG

RECESSED PLATE IN SOLE TAKES PEG IN END OF LEG

ENLARGED DETAIL

A PORTABLE STOOL

The cook and the navigator need a seat some of the time, as does the owner's wife when she is making-up in front of her mirror – if the boat is big enough for a dressing table. This stool has the virtues of simplicity and steadiness. Its four legs are well splayed out and they each have a bronze peg which lodges firmly in a brass plate let into the cabin sole. There can be several sets of these plates so that the stool can be used in different positions.

By having the legs and ties of the same section, cutting and planing the wood is simplified. The seat frame can be the same, or perhaps of the same thickness but a greater depth than shown here.

The seat can be flat, but the cold-moulded curvaceous one shown is more comfortable and elegant. It can have a fitted cushion, in which case the edge framing on the ply is not needed because the ply is entirely covered by the cushion material.

A SEAT FOR GALLEY OR CHART TABLE . . . OR BOTH

It is a great advantage to be able to sit down to work, and this seat has all sorts of special assets. It stows away quickly and unobtrusively, like a drawer. When needed, its holding clip (not shown in the sketch) is released and it is simply pulled out. The end is pushed through a slot in the galley front and dropped down so that the lip prevents the seat sliding back.

Being narrow, it can be sat on in the ordinary way, or astride. It must be as long as the gap between galley and chart table, and if it is to have enough room to stow away horizontally it will be important to have the chart table fairly near the centreline of the yacht. The seat slides on runners like a drawer when it is pushed into its stowed position, and the end lip must be made so that it is easy to grip, or, alternatively, an end handle must be screwed on.

The section shows a light, strong assembly, but solid wood can be used, or a solid plank with a single stiffener or pair of them on the bottom. Whatever method is used to build up this seat, glue and metal fastenings are needed, and when ply is used the edges should be covered as shown.

LIGHT HOLLOW SEAT

ENLARGED SECT<u>N</u> AT A-A

MARINE PLY ¼ INCH ~ 6mm

1 INCH ~ 50mm

½ INCH ~ 12 mm

BETWEEN 6 AND 8 INCHES ~ 150 AND 200 MM

2 INCHES - 50MM

GALLEY

CHART TABLE

SEAT SLIDES ACROSS

DRAWER

A

A

SEAT STOWED

LOOKING AFT OR FORWARD

END OF SEAT HOOKS OVER

CABIN SOLE

CHART TABLE FRONT NEARER BOATS CENTRE-LINE THAN GALLEY

ELEVN

2 INCHES
50 MM

¾ INCH
20MM

1½ INCHES
40 MM

JOINT GLUED
AND SCREWᴰ

SECTION

GAP FOR
CLEANING

BARREL BOLT HOLDS BAR UP

SAFETY BAR IN STOWED POSITᴺ

3×1½ INCH~75×40ᴹ SAFETY
BAR IN OPERATING POSITION

DEEP TROUGH
FOR STOWAGE

ABOUT 24 INCHES~600ᴹᴹ

2½ INCHES~60ᴹᴹ

8 INCHES~200 MM OR TO
SUIT NAVIGATOR

SIDE DOOR ENSURE LOCKER
IS ACCESSIBLE AT ALL TIMES

SEE ENLARGED DETAIL
OF TOE-RAIL ABOVE

LOCKER

Ian Nicolson.

LOOKING AFT
AT FORWARD FACING
NAVIGATORS SEAT

CURVED SEAT FOR THE NAVIGATOR

Boats heel but navigators like to be upright, so a shaped seat by the chart table is popular. To keep the navigator safe, a bar which drops down and prevents him falling off the seat is a sensible precaution, provided it is strong enough to stand up to severe conditions. One end of this bar has a pivot bolt through a pair of short lengths of angle-bar on a bulkhead. The other end drops into a deep socket, or has a metal ring which hooks into a snap shackle or similar securing device.

Access to the locker under the seat should be from the side, otherwise the navigator has to be disturbed if the locker entrance is at the top.

To help the navigator stay in place, there is a toe rail (like a wood fiddle) inboard of his foot rest. This wood batten must stop short at the ends otherwise a puddle may accumulate outboard of it; the end gaps are also helpful when cleaning.

TOP YACHT'S TOILET

The ideas here were seen in a Camper and Nicholson 46-footer. The wc is an electric one, hidden when not in use under a cork covered seat hinged down from the bulkhead. To deal with an electrical failure, the wc has a diaphragm type pump concealed in a locker so that it is easy to get at when it needs servicing.

The adjacent locker has a shelf with an upper shelf to form a safe storage for cosmetics; this upper shelf is of perspex and the 'cut-outs' fit the shape of the different containers and bottles. If, after a few years or even months, different cosmetics are bought, a new perspex panel with the appropriately shaped holes can be substituted.

CORK SEAT COVERING

MARINE PLY

REBATED TEAK EDGING & HANDLE

WHITE FORMICA

ENLARGED DETAIL AT Z-Z

PERSPEX FIDDLE

PERSPEX SHELF

LOCKER FOR PUMP, PIPING ETC.

TURN-BUTTON HOLDS SEAT UP

LOCKER FOR TOILET GEAR

HAND PUMP FOR WHEN POWER FAILS

CUT-OUT HOLES FIT COSMETIC BOTTLES

VIEW AT 'Y'

FOLDING SEAT OVER ELECTRIC W.C.

Ian Nicolson

BOW-FRONTED COVER CONCEALS ELECTRIC W.C. AND GIVES EXTRA FOOT-ROOM EACH SIDE

VIEW LOOKING OUTBOARD

T-SHAPED HINGE HAS AT LEAST THREE
3/16 INCH~5 MM BOLTS IN EACH LEAF

SAFETY BAR HAS WELL ROUNDED EDGES

ENLARGED DETAIL

BARREL BOLT HOLDS SAFETY
BAR IN UP POSITION

BULKHEAD

DOUBLER PAD

THIS DISTANCE ABOUT
3 INCHES~75 MM BUT
MAKE TO SUIT BOAT

HANDRAIL

SAFETY BAR IN
LOWERED POSITION

Z

THIS DISTANCE ABOUT
9 INCHES~225 MM BUT
MAKE TO SUIT BOAT

BARREL BOLT HOLDS
SAFETY BAR IN
LOWERED POSITION

W.C.

Ian Nicolson

SAFETY BAR ABOUT 3×2 INCHES
75×50 MM HINGED AT OTHER END

SUPPORT CHOCK ABOUT
5×4×1 INCH~125×100×25 MM

ENLARGED DETAIL. VIEW AT Z

TOILET GUARD BAR

There is nothing funny about being pitched off the wc as the boat lurches over a wave top. This folding guard bar prevents that sort of accident.

It consists of a strong bar, here made of wood though a metal tube can be used, with one end hinged to the bulkhead on one side of the wc. When in use the bar folds across to the opposite bulkhead, where its end rests in a recessed wood chock. To lock it down, there is a common barrel bolt, and another of these holds the bar in the upright, open position.

The precise position of the bar relative to the toilet seat height needs discovering by trial and error, as the height of the seat from the cabin sole has to be taken into account, as does the total space inside the toilet compartment.

TOILET COMPARTMENT INTO BOUDOIR

A small change can make an ordinary toilet cabin into a place where men can shave in comfort, and women can spend time making-up. The essential addition is a comfortable seat and this may be fitted so that it hinges down over the wc. When the seat is up against the wall the wc is back in use and the toilet paper is handy, fixed to the underside of the hinged seat.

The seat, when it is in use, should be close to the top of the wc otherwise it will be too high for comfort, especially for small people. The mirror should extend right down to the level of the vanity unit and be 3ft (1m) high.

GAPS BETWEEN BATTONS ⅜ INCH ~ 10 M

PLAN VIEW AT 'A'

BULKHEAD

TURN-BUTTON

MIRROR

VANITY UNIT

HINGED SEAT OVER W.C.

TOILET PAPER

SEE ENLARGED DETAIL

HARD-WOOD SEAT BATTENS 1½ × ⅝ INCHES ~ 40 × 15 M IN SECTION

THREE TIE PIECES OF SAME SECTION AS BATTENS

END LEDGES 1¼ × 1 INCH ~ 30 × 25 M

ENLARGED DETAIL

TOP EYEPLATES [PORT & STARBOARD] FOR SAFETY LINES BOLTED TO LOWER ONES WHICH SUPPORT WIRES

RETAINING CLIP

CURTAIN

TOILET SLID AFT TO STOWED POSITION

COCKPIT WELL

WOOD CHOCK

STEP-SEAT HINGES UP WHEN TOILET IS IN USE

PLASTIC COVERED WIRE ⅛ INCH ~3MM DIAMETER

BACK-FLAP HINGES 2 INCHES~ 50ᴹᴹ LONG~ 8 BOLTS EACH

Ian Nicolson.

WOOD BASE ON TWIN SLIDES

STOPS AT SAIL TRACK ENDS

PARALLEL LENGTHS OF SAIL TRACK FOR SLIDES

FLEXIBLE PIPING ALLOWS W.C. TO SLIDE FORWARD INTO CABIN

SAIL TRACK BOLTED TO SOLE BEARERS

TUCKED-AWAY TOILET

On a small boat, it's absurd to use up a great chunk of the limited available cabin space for the toilet. This compartment is only in use for a short time each day, and as it needs headroom, it tends to take up valuable space.

By putting the wc on a pair of slides it can be pushed under the cockpit out of the way when not in use. Smells go up out of the main hatch swiftly, and the seacocks can be handy, the inlet one being combined perhaps with a cockpit drain.

That folding step makes an excellent seat but it must have a clip to hold it in the up position. Its top surface will probably be covered with Treadmaster or a similar slip-proof surface. The two lines of sail track on the sole are tough enough to stand up to all sorts of rough use, but will need a little lubrication. On the wc's wood base there must be a barrel bolt which locks the wc in the stowed or in-use position as required.

PULL-OUT BASIN OVER WC

One of the advantages of a basin arranged like a drawer is that it can be large, with ample space either side for washing gear, false teeth and so on. The drawer must have strong smooth slides and common sail track is ideal for this. To hold the basin, either when stowed away under the side-deck or pulled out so that one of the crew can wash, there must be some locking device. Usually this is a simple barrel bolt, as shown top left.

Piping for the drain and water supply must be flexible and long enough to extend to the 'pulled-out' and 'closed' positions of the basin. It is usual to have the drain flattened at its bottom end and tucked under the wc seat, so when the basin plug is pulled out the dirty water runs into the wc bowl.

DOUBLER GLUED AND SCREWED TO BULKHEAD

BARREL BOLT HOLDS DRAWER

SAIL TRACK WITH PAIR OF LONG SLIDES SCREWED UPWARDS INTO BASIN DRAWER

MOULDING OVER PLY EDGE

BASIN HELD BY NUMEROUS SCREWS INTO WOOD DOUBLER

PULL-OUT DRAWER CONTAINS WASH-BASIN

ENLARGED DETAIL
OTHER END OF DRAWER IS THE SAME

BULKHEAD

SEE ENLARGED DETAIL

VIEW LOOKING OUTBOARD

PULL-OUT DRAWER SLIDES OUTBOARD WHEN W.C. IS IN USE

FLEXIBLE DRAIN RUNS INTO W.C. BOWL UNDER LAVATORY SEAT

BACKING BLOCK FOR WOOD SCREW ENDS

BULKHEAD OR FURNITURE FRONT

HARD-WOOD BATTEN COVERS P.V.C. EDGES

Ian Nicolson

SLOPE ENSURES PROMPT DRAINAGE

P.V.C. BACK

END OF TOILET ROLL

P.V.C. "BOX" KEEPS PAPER DRY

EASILY REMOVABLE ROPE HAS ELEGANT KNOT ON TOP AND HALF HITCH ON BOTTOM

WOOD BAR FORMS AXLE FOR TOILET ROLL

ENDS OF P.V.C. "BOX" DOUBLED FOR EXTRA STIFFNESS

KEEPING THE TOILET PAPER DRY

The open-bottomed container for keeping toilet paper dry, even in gale conditions when drips come through the overhead vent, is stitched together by a sailmaker out of PVC cloth, so it never needs painting or varnishing. It weighs very little, and if anyone is flung against it in rough weather, they will not be bruised.

The horizontal rod can be made of metal tubing, or a wood or plastic bar. It can have a screwed-on end, as well as the fixed end, or the seamanlike 'split pin' shown here made of a short length of thin rope with a decorative knot on top and a single half hitch at the bottom to prevent the rope coming out by accident.

If the bulkhead is the usual thin ply, screws will either be too short, or they will protrude right through. This explains why there has to be a backing block.

EMPTYING A WIDE FLAT BILGE

In a boat with no deep sump in the bilge, water under the cabin sole slops about over a wide area. When the boat heels, the puddle of bilge water migrates outboard, further and further as the angle of heel increases.

Two techniques are available to deal with this situation. The top drawing shows a single large bilge pump with suctions fixed athwartships at different points to deal with various angles of heel. The suctions are led to a manifold which is a metal box with a row of valves, one for each suction. Normally, only one valve will be open at once.

The second arrangement need not cost more, in fact, such is the cost of valves and longer runs of piping, it may be cheaper. A row of pumps is fixed on a bulkhead, port and starboard. Each pump has its own suction line and can have its own discharge, though in the drawing there are outlet manifolds each side, each taking three outlets. If there is a lot of water in the bilge, and if the person pumping does not have to hang on for safety with one hand, he can operate two of these small pumps at once.

SINGLE LARGE BILGE PUMP

OUTLET PIPE LED UP NEAR DECK

DISCHARGE WITH SEACOCK HIGH UP

STRUM BOXES MUST BE FIXED IN PLACE

SUCTION MANIFOLD

SINGLE PUMP SYSTEM

STRUM BOXES SPREAD OUT ATHWARTSHIPS

AS PUMPS ARE CLOSE TWO CAN BE WORKED AT ONCE

SEACOCK AND SKIN FITTING

Ian Nicolsa.

OUTLET MANIFOLD

STRAIGHT EASY PIPING

SMALL BILGE PUMPS SEPARATELY PIPED IN

SEPARATE SUCTIONS EACH WITH A STRUM BOX

MULTI-PUMP SYSTEM

PORT AND STARBOARD SIDES MATCH

AIR PIPE

STOWAGE UNDER SETTEE

LONG FLAT TANK

FILLER PIPE

SALOON SETTEE

TANK UNDER SOLE WITH
ALL PIPE CONNECTIONS
AT ONE END

Ian Nicolson

AIR PIPE

METAL FLANGE WITH BOLTS
THROUGH SOLE BEARERS

FILLER PIPE ELBOW

DRAW-OFF PIPE ELBOW

METAL TANGS AT
EACH SOLE BEARER
BOLTED THROUGH

TANK END
ENLARGED DETAIL

EXTRA TANKAGE

On any cruiser, it is almost impossible to have too much tank capacity. Often when an old boat is examined it will be found that for every ten years of her life, the capacity of both fuel and water tanks has been increased by 20 per cent and sometimes even by 50 per cent. One way to get more capacity is to fit flat stainless steel tanks in otherwise unwanted spaces, such as below the cabin sole, at the bottom of the settee lockers, and in those areas too often made damp by bilge water.

These tanks should be firmly secured along the whole of two edges at least, with an absolute minimum of six bolts per tank. The bolts should be $1/4$in (6mm) diameter for every 20ft, (6m) of boat length, and the tanks they go through should be at least twice as strong as the bolts. The tanks should also rest on semi-soft packing such as wood or a dense foam plastic material – never on fibreglass.

The important feature of this sort of tank is that for installation reasons, it is almost always best to have all the pipe connections at one end, and all in the form of elbows, so that the joining plastic pipes run off parallel with the end plate.

FUEL PROBLEMS SOLVED

When refuelling, it's hard to avoid some splashes round the filler pipe, and from there the contamination goes all over the boat, on deck and below. The preventative arrangement shown here is seen sometimes on large motor-cruisers but can be used on the smallest boat.

Each filler pipe is fitted in a stainless steel box with enough space all round the pipe for old newspapers or rags to be spread. Drips during refuelling are blotted up by the paper or rags and disposed of ashore. The cap on the filler is fully watertight and is doubly protected as the surrounding box keeps water away from the filler. If water does get in, or if there is condensation in the drip-well the little drain hole located half way up lets the water escape.

The same type of filler can be used for water, and if the pipe is kept straight it is easy to use a dip-stick. Some people prefer a sight glass, as shown at the fore end of the tank, but of course both dip-stick and sight glass have to be used intelligently if the fuel tank bottom slopes.

DRIP WELLS SHOWN SHADED [LIDS REMOVED]

WATER TANK FILLER

BARS ON FILLER CAPS FOR EASY UNSCREWING

FUEL TANK FILLER

PLAN VIEW

ENLARGED DETAIL AT Z

HINGED LID IS SEMI-WATERTIGHT

SCREW-ON CAP WITH WATER-TIGHT WASHER

STAINLESS STEEL DRIP-WELL

DOUBLY ENLARGED DETAIL OF FILLER CAP

STAINLESS STEEL DRIP WELL

STRAIGHT FILLER PIPE ALLOWS DIP-STICK TO BE USED EASILY

DRAIN HOLE ¼ INCH ~6MM DIAMETER

FUEL OR WATER FILLER PIPE

COCKPIT WELL

FORWARD

BREATHER PIPE

IF TANK BOTTOM SLOPES A DIP-STICK GIVES A MISLEADING READING

SIGHT GLASS SHOWS LEVEL OF FLUID IN TANK

CABIN TOP DECK

TYPICAL WIDTH OF REFUELLING LOCKER IS 12 INCHES ~ 300 MM

LONG-TAILED HINGES BOLTED ON

HASP HOLDS LID DOWN AGAINST VANDALS & GALES

FORE & AFT LENGTH ABOUT 18 INCHES ~ 450 MM

DRAIN-PIPE LEADS OVERBOARD BELOW W-LINE

OIL-TIGHT BULKHD

TOMMY BAR WELDED ON CAP

FUEL OR WATER TANK FILLER PIPE

AIR PIPE TO TANK

SEA-COCK IN ACCESSIBLE POSITION

Ian Nicolson

CLEAN REFUELLING

Fuel is smelly and it has a bad habit of staining whatever it touches. Wet fuel left on a deck attracts grit and it is hard to take fuel on board without spilling at least a few drips.

Having a special locker for fuel filling pipes reduces a lot of complications besides making it easier to keep a boat clean and pleasant. The locker may be let into the side of a cabin top, perhaps with an adjacent locker for the gas cylinders. When this locker is washed out the water must drain overboard via a special pipe which comes out below the waterline, with its own seacock.

Washing out is not started until as much of the spilt fuel as possible has been mopped up with rags or paper. The filler pipe cap has to be put on before washing out starts, and even if a lot of water is swilling around inside the locker, none will get down this important pipe because it is raised above deck level. To make it easy to take the filler cap off, there is a stout rod welded across the top which is gently tapped to make the cap unscrew.

SOLID FUEL STOVE I

Nothing makes a cabin more cosy than a good solid fuel stove. It can be kept burning low all day and all night yet it gives out enough heat to warm a big area, and may even feed a batch of radiators run from a back boiler.

All during the planning and fitting of a stove, the risk of fire has to be remembered. Also, a stove is heavy, so it needs a strong base which will stay put whichever way the yacht happens to tip. Before designing the base it is best to buy, or at least measure, the stove so as to get the outside dimensions, the feet bolt centres, the location of the chimney relative to the front face and so on.

The base has to be secured to the hull with a big factor of safety (quite six or eight times) and the stove should be positioned so that a straight chimney can be installed unless there is a very strong reason why this cannot be achieved. Ideally, the chimney should be in one length. No drying rail should be set low down otherwise clothing may rest against the hot stove when the boat is heeling, and a fire result.

INSULATING COLLAR

UP-TAKE THROUGH CABIN TOP DECK, NOT SIDE-DECK

RAIL FOR DRYING TOWELS ETC.

A STRAIGHT UP-TAKE IS BEST AND CHEAPEST

GUARD MADE OF PERFORATED METAL OR MESH TO PREVENT BURNT HANDS AND CLOTHES

MARINE TYPE SOLID FUEL STOVE

RELIABLE SELF-CLOSING HASPS ON ALL STOVE DOORS

METAL TRAY WITH FIDDLE ALL ROUND 4 INCHES ~ 100 MM HIGH

FLANGED METAL BRACKETS KEEP STOVE CLEAR OF HULL

TOWEL RAILS ETC. ARE DANGEROUS AT STOVE LEVEL

AT LEAST FOUR BOLTS WITH LOCKED NUTS

LARGE PERFORATIONS HELP WARM AIR TO CIRCULATE AND KEEP HULL COOL

Ian Nicolson

FIRE EXTINGUISHER AT LEAST 2KG ~ 4½ LBS SIZE

METAL SUPPORT FOR UP-TAKE GUARD

ELECTRIC FAN IN TRUNKING

ABOUT 6 FEET ~ 2 METRES BETWⁿ STOVE & FIRE EXTINGR

WARM AIR

SAFETY BAR DOUBLE-LOCKS ALL STOVE DOORS WHEN AT SEA

BULKHEAD

IF A BLANKET FALLS OFF A SETTEE IT MUST BE WELL CLEAR OF STOVE

METAL PANEL

FUEL STOWED WELL CLEAR OF STOVE

1 INCH ~ 25ᴹ AIR GAP

Ian Nicolson

GAP BETWEEN FURNITURE WITH UPHOLSTERY AND STOVE 24 INCHES ~ 600MM OR MORE

GAP BETWEEN STOVE AND BULKHEAD 15 INCHES ~ 375MM OR MORE

SOLID FUEL STOVE II

Insulating washers should be put under the stove feet to prevent heat reaching the support base. Nearby furniture and bulkheads must be protected either by distance, or heat-resisting materials. Another safety factor is the fire extinguisher, which should be just handy, but not right where a fire is likely to occur.

To use some of the ample heat which comes from a stove, a trunked fan can suck air from inside the chimney guard and feed it into the next cabin. This technique can be used on its own, or to supplement a back boiler feeding radiators in adjacent cabins.

The technique whereby the stove is in one cabin and the chimney led through another works well but needs very careful insulation and is not cheap to do.

CHIMNEY INSULATOR

The chimney rising up from a solid fuel stove is hot, and can easily damage the cabin top deck unless there is some way of insulating the structure from the flue. An old-fashioned protector is the water trough, welded round the chimney. The trough is kept full of seawater and this evaporates, so that it has to be replenished every so often. Replenishment may be by a drip feed from a tank on deck, or by a hose from a marina tap, set to drip into the trough.

In wet weather rain will fill the trough, but possibly not fast enough. At sea it may be a problem refilling the trough, unless there is enough spray slicing in over the weather rail to top up the water as it evaporates.

WATER NEEDS REGULAR TOPPING UP

HARDWOOD CHOCK

BOLTED FLANGE

CABIN TOP DECK

Ian Nicolson

INSULATION TROUGH RIGHT ROUND

HOT STOVE PIPE

SMOKE FROM CABIN STOVE

TROUGH OF ⅛ INCH ~ 3MM THICK METAL

EIGHT ¼ INCH ~ 5MM DIAMETER BOLTS

BREATHER PIPE

SMALL HOT WATER TANK
EASILY TOPPED UP

SMALL BORE HOT WATER
CIRCULATING PIPES

STANDARD ELECTRIC PUMP

PORTABLE HEATING
COIL OF PIPING

FLOW

BOAT'S COOKER

SMALL RADIATORS OR
PIPES IN ACCOMMODATION

BOAT'S ELECTRICAL SUPPLY

SIMPLE CENTRAL HEATING

The attraction of this cabin heating arrangement is that it is easily made up using standard components which are widely available and cheap. To keep corrosion down, fresh water should be used in the circuit, and the components should not be of mild steel, except perhaps the holding tank. If this is of steel it should be galvanized or painted using epoxy resins.

Apart from short joining lengths, the piping should not be of plastic as this softens when hot water passes through it. Stainless steel, brass or copper piping can be used, and can be made up into radiators by bending in a zig-zag manner.

The heating unit must be able to stand up to 'cooking' on the galley stove. If the coil is kept flat it may be possible to cook a meal at the same time and on the same burner. Once the water in the circuit has been heated it can be pumped round for some time, gently warming the cabin, without further heating. The best flow rate, like every other aspect of this system will need to be discovered by experimentation, and will depend on the size of the circuit, the pipe diameter, and so on. But in general, the smallest size of standard yacht pump is likely to be adequate.

STOWAGE BY THE COMPANION WAY

At the cabin exit everyone needs simple stowage racks for those items which are needed in a hurry. Different people have varying ideas about the equipment which should be stowed here, but the articles which are illustrated cover many crises. The fiddle with 'cut-outs' is a shelf set above the main shelf, with sawn out shapes to fit the tools etc.

The best kind of rack has room for additional things in future years. A deep shelf underneath for lengths of line, extra sail tiers or maybe a bar of chocolate and so on is also a good idea. If the fuse box, with its numerous switches, is also built into the same unit, this will often save money and make this piece of furniture look purposeful, sensible and decorative.

Making the inside edge of the shelves into a grab-rail and protector against errant spray is common sense. The grab-rail could be continued further down to help anyone wriggling into the quarter berth.

FLARE

FIRE EXTINGUISHER

KNIFE

SCREWDRIVER

PLIERS SPIKE & SHACKLE OPENER

VIEW AT 'A-A'

FLASH-LIGHT ETC.

SHELF FOR ODDMENTS

FUSEBOX

GRAB-RAIL

FIDDLE WITH "CUT-OUTS"

PERSPEX FIDDLES

A

A

FLASH-LIGHT

FIDDLE WITH "CUT-OUTS"

GRAB-RAIL ALSO FORMS SPRAY-GUARD

HIGH PERSPEX FIDDLE ON SHELF

FUSE-BOX HAS HINGED FRONT

CABIN STEPS

QUARTER BERTH

Ian Nicolson

LOOKING AFT

SECTION AT 'A-A'

TWO SCREWS EACH SIDE
AT FORE END ONLY

TOPSIDES

HARDWOOD
2 × 1½ INCHES
40 × 40 MM

3 × 1½ OZ. CHOPPED
STRAND MAT

FORE END OF SHELF

2 INCH ~ 50 MM VENT HOLES AT
8 INCH ~ 200 M CENTRES

SOFT-WOOD FILLET 1×1INCH~25×25 M

ENLARGED DETAILS

SCREWS AT 6 INCH ~ 150 M CENTRES

HARDWOOD TRIM GLUED NOT SCREWED

SEE ENLARGED
DETAIL

SOFT PANNIER FIXED
TO BOAT'S SIDE

AT LEAST
13 INCHES
330 MM

A

A

QUARTER BERTH MATTRESS

Ian Nicolson.

SHELF WITH DEEP FIDDLE

SHELF LENGTH
NOT OVER 28 INCHES ~
700 MM

◄━━ FORWARD ►

VIEW LOOKING OUTBOARD

STOWAGE ROUND A QUARTER BERTH

A shelf over the foot of a quarter berth uses up otherwise unwanted space. The shelf must not be so low that it fouls the feet of the sleeper, nor should it extend so far forward that it makes turning over on the berth impossible. A low fiddle is needed to keep kitbags on the shelf, as shown at top right. If the fiddle is just glued then no dowelling is needed. Vent holes are advisable on the shelf. The sides of the shelf are supported by glassed over triangular section pieces, shown top left. The shelf is only screwed each side at the forward end then it is easy to take out for cleaning. Forward of the shelf, there is space usually for a book rack or high fiddled shelf, and at the top of the berth a large bag secured to the side of the boat gives a lot of storage. If clothes are kept in this waterproofed bag, the sleeper can lie comfortably against it even when the boat is banging about in a seaway.

BIG BOTTLES

The trend towards buying drink in bigger bottles can make life difficult for anyone arranging suitable stowage space. However, the lower part of many clothes hanging lockers can be used without stealing important capacity because it is at the top of these lockers that a good fore-and-aft length is needed. A particular advantage of this bottle rack is that it is safe in rough weather, yet the hooch is close at hand and does not have to be delved for in deep, dark, dank caverns.

Normally, the bottle rack will be made off the boat, and fitted with a wood rim all round which is bolted or screwed to the bulkhead. The access hole must not be so large that it weakens a strength bulkhead and it should have rounded corners with a radius of at least 3in (75mm). The slots, if large enough for $1^1/_2$-litre bottles, will also hold big *Coca Cola* bottles, soda water containers and so on.

ALLOW 4¼ INCHES~105 M DIAMETER & 14 INCHES~350 M HEIGHT FOR 1½ LITRE BOTTLES

SHAPED FIDDLES ⅝ INCH~15 M THICK

PLAN VIEW

CLOTHES LOCKER

BOX FORMS CAVE LOCKER

A   A

END OF SETTEE BERTH

SHELF IN CLOTHES LOCKER

SPACE FOR 1½ LITRE BOTTLES

GAP 13 INCHES~325 mm HIGH

6 INCHES~125 MM

SETTEE CUSHION

SECTION AT A-A LOOKING OUTBOARD

FORWARD

MINIMUM INSIDE
WIDTH 5 INCHES
125 MM

LOCKER FOR
WET CLOTHES

FORE-AND-AFT
DIVISIONS AT
UNEVEN SPACES

PLAN VIEW

DRY STOWAGE FOR TOWELS,
KITCHEN PAPER ROLLS, ETC.

RACK FOR GLASSES
AND SOFT DRINKS

FIRST AID EQUIPMENT & TOILET GEAR

WATER-PROOF HINGES KEEP OUT DRIPS

TOILET ROLLS & WASH BAGS ETC.

BOOKSHELF
FULL WIDTH
ATHWARTPS

RACK FOR MAGAZINE & LIFEJACKET
STOWAGE OPEN AFT INTO THE SALOON

BOTTLE LOCKER OPENS INTO SALOON

ELEVATION LOOKING
TO PORT

STOWAGE BETWEEN DOUBLE BULKHEADS

It is usual for the bulkhead between the saloon and toilet to support the mast, so a double bulkhead here, for extra strength is a special asset. It can also act as a sound barrier, which plenty of owners and their girl friends favour, for extra privacy.

If the gap between the bulkheads is made into lockers and shelves, some should open forwards, some aft, to get the best use from the space. It makes sense for each member for the crew to have his own personal locker for toilet gear near the basin, and everyone wants a drip-proof locker for the toilet roll, but there is a limit to the amount of gear which can be conveniently stowed in the toilet compartment.

The top of the space can be used as a ventilator box, and part of it can be a vent trunk to the bilge, or a chimney for the cabin stove.

UNOBTRUSIVE STOWAGE

It is common practice to fix fire extinguishers onto bulkheads, where they can be seen easily. Sometimes other safety gear such as big flashlights, those outsize foghorns and even life jackets are secured up in prominent positions where they can be grabbed in a hurry. If there is a shortage of bulkhead space, or if the owner wants to keep all his weight low down, or if gear screwed up on a bulkhead is going to bruise the crew in rough weather, alternative sites have to be found.

One good ploy is to indent the front of a settee or berth and have the safety gear secured in brackets in the recess. Here it is out of the way but easily reached. The space used is small, and the cost of arranging this type of stowage is minimal. Only if the equipment is heavy is it necessary to have support pillars behind the recess.

BERTH BASE

ENLARGED DETAIL

CLEATING PIECE 2 × 1½ INCHES ~ 50 × 40MM

SCREWS 1¾ INCH 10 GAUGE

ONE OR TWO PILLARS 2 × 1 INCH ~ 50 × 25MM

OUTBOARD

Ian Nicolson

SETTEE BERTH CUSHION

FIBREGLASS CASING OR PLASTIC BOWL

FIRE EXTINGUISHER OR LARGE TORCH OR FOG-HORN ETC.

AT LEAST TWO SPRING BRACKETS OR SIMILAR

SETTEE FRONT CUT AWAY TO TAKE CASING

EXCEPT FOR SMALL FIRE EXTINGUISHERS TWO PILLARS ARE NEEDED HERE

ENLARGED DETAIL

SETTEE BERTH TOP

3/16 INCH~5MM BOLTS AT ABOUT 5 INCH~125MM CENTRES

1¼ INCHES
30MM — TAPERED FINGER HOLE

WATER-TIGHT LID OF PLASTIC BOX

SIDE OF PLASTIC BOX

REBATED OR LAMINATED
WOOD SECTION

LIFT-OFF LID

STANDARD PLASTIC
BOX GIVES WATER-
TIGHT STOWAGE

THREE LAYERS 1½ OZ.
CHOPPED STRAND MAT AT ENDS

Ian Nicolson

WHERE LARGE PIECES OF SETTEE BASE
ARE CUT OUT PROPS ARE NEEDED

SECTION LOOKING FORWARD OR AFT

DRY UNDER-BERTH STOWAGE

Plastic boxes are cheap, easy to clean, available in many sizes and easy to replace. They make excellent storage containers because they are watertight and light. For use under berth tops, the kind with a lip all round is easy to fit using either rebated wood, or wood glued and bolted up in 'steps' as shown in the enlarged detail. It is usual to buy the biggest size of box which will fit the available space, and have a row of them the full length of the cavity under the berth. Bilge water can slop up in large dollops without wetting the gear stowed in the boxes. If the berth base is of fibreglass and a lot of it is cut away for access to the boxes, some compensating structure must be added to prevent the berth top collapsing when a heavy person sits on it. This reinforcing can consist of battens secured along the underside, or props as shown here.
Alternatively, a combination of props and stringers can be used.

STOWAGE BINS ABOVE THE BILGE WATER

This is yet another way of using watertight plastic boxes to keep gear dry. Even if the boat inverts, clothes, food, batteries and so on should stay safe in that strong polythene style of box which has a tightly fitting lid.

By having pairs or sets of three or even four angle brackets under each box, the space beneath can still be used for gear which can get wet without worry. However, some shipwrights will prefer to make a fore-and-aft support, using perhaps a plank set on edge, the top taking the load of the plastic boxes and the bottom lying snug on the inside of the hull. Such a plank would be glassed over with four runs of $1\frac{1}{2}$oz chopped strand mat along each side, swept well up and down the hull.

The securing of the boxes must be such that the through bolts do not tear through the plastic, so the internal wood pad is essential and should be nearly as deep as the box, and almost as long fore-and-aft.

ENLARGED DETAIL

DISTANCE PIECE NEEDED TO GET BOX LID OFF

LID OF PLASTIC BOX

INTERNAL WOOD PAD FORMS WASHER PLATE

BERTH FRONT

AT LEAST FOUR BOLTS MINIMUM DIAMETER 3/16 INCH ~ 5 MM

BERTH TOP PANEL LIFTS OUT FOR ACCESS

SEE ENLARGED DETAIL ABOVE

CABIN SOLE

BILGE WATER RUNS HARMLESSLY PAST STORAGE BOX

STANDARD PLASTIC BOX OR ROW OF THEM ~ LARGEST SIZE WHICH WILL FIT

TWO OR MORE BRACKETS UNDER LARGE OR HEAVILY LOADED BOXES

BOLTS

ENLARGED DETAILS

SETTEE TOPS

LOCKER LID

SIDE OF P.V.C. CONTAINER

LOCKER LID

SIDE OF P.V.C. CONTAINER

SCREWS AT 4 INCH ~ 100 M/M CENTRES

SETTEE WITH CUSHION AND LOCKER LID REMOVED

SEE ENLARGED DETAILS

SETTEE FRONT

CABIN SOLE

P.V.C. CONTAINER WITH WATER-PROOFED STITCHING

VENT SLOT AND HAND-HOLE EACH END

Ian Nicolson

WATER SLOSHES UP HERE

CONTAINERS BELOW SETTEE

Lift off a settee cushion, take away the locker lids, and there is a large and very useful locker. Unfortunately, if there is even a tiny quantity of water in the bilge, it invades the settee locker when the boat heels, especially if the bilge is shallow.

To avoid wet gear, suspended containers are fitted under the settee top. These containers can be made of many materials, but PVC as used to make sail covers is a favourite. It is light, waterproof, easily made up by a local sailmaker, and it needs no painting or finishing treatment apart from the application of a waterproofing compound along the stitched joins.

In the top drawings two alternative methods of securing the containers is shown. To use the one on the right the container must have a slot each end for reaching through to hold the wood in place while the screws are put in. The left hand sketch shows a technique whereby the wood strips are first bolted under the settee, then the container screwed to the wood, so no slots are needed in the container.

UNDER SOLE STOWAGE

Stowage is seldom adequate in the galley, so though it smacks of desperation, there is justification for using the space below the sole as a store. Containers which fit exactly between the sole bearers usually have to be specially made, which explains why some owners have the bearers shifted, to suit standard boxes and baskets.

The type of plastic-covered wire basket sold for deep freezes, shown top left, is popular though its ledges are at the ends, which usually means special lips may have to be fitted each side to lodge on flanges on the bearers. These flanges should be of hardwood, glued and screwed at 5in (125mm) intervals.

Some people use plywood panels fixed on the undersides of the bearers, with round holes cut in the ply to take standard plastic buckets. It always pays to buy the containers first, before making up the arrangements to support them. The hatches in the sole must be fairly small and easily portable. If there is one big sole hatch the cook will have great difficulty picking it up to get at the food stowed below.

COOK STANDS ON THIS HATCH TO LIFT OTHER ONE AND VICE VERSA

VIEW ATHWARTSHIPS IN GALLEY

EACH HATCH MUST WEIGH LESS THAN 25 LBS-10 KGS

GALLEY SOLE

SOLE BEARER

INTERNAL HANDLE FOLDED DOWN

SOLE BEARER

TOP OF KEEL

SPACE FOR BILGE-WATER

STANDARD FREEZER WIRE BASKET 21½×11½×7 INCHES~540×290×175 MM

SPECIALLY MADE BOX OF WOOD METAL OR FIBRE-GLASS FITS EXACTLY

RECESSED SOLE LIFTING EYE BOLTED DOWN

Ian Nicolson

ENLARGED DETAIL

STANDARD PLASTIC BUCKET ABOUT 10 INCHES~250 M DIAMETER AT THE TOP BUT CAN BE SQUASHED TO ABOUT 9 INCHES~225 M

ORIGINAL EXTERNAL HANDLE MAY HAVE TO BE REMOVED AND A NEW ROPE ONE FITTED

DECORATIVE HEAD SCREWS

HARDWOOD BACKING STRIP TYPICALLY 1 × 5/8 INCHES ~ 25 × 15 MM

SMALL PLASTIC BOX FORMS STOWAGE SHELF

AMPLE SPACE NEEDED BETWEEN BOXES TO GET GEAR INTO LOWER ONE

LARGE PLASTIC BOX WITH DRAIN-HOLES IN BOTTOM

Ian Nicolson.

LEDGE PIECE TYPICALLY 3/4 × 3/4 INCH ~ 20 × 20 MM SECTION HARDWOOD

LOCKER DOOR

QUICK AND CHEAP EXTRA STOWAGE

There are few schemes which give cheaper extra stowage than the fitting of plastic boxes inside locker doors. These boxes can also be located under settees, in cockpit lockers beneath the seats, fixed inside oilskin lockers high up where there is often a little space clear of the hanging oilskins, and so on.

Plastic boxes are available in a great variety of sizes from hardware stores, camping shops, industrial suppliers and so on. They need no painting, and are waterproof. Because the material is soft there must by a wood batten to take the screws or bolts which support each box. A second wood batten along the bottom is only needed if there are to be lots of heavy items in the box, or if the box is longer than about 12in (300mm). If in doubt, fit a base support to be safe.

Before fitting one or more of these boxes inside a locker door, the hinges should be checked. Usually, the weak point here is the size of the screws and by changing to bolts the hinges can be made to support the extra load.

FRESH FOOD STORAGE

In the days before fridges, fresh vegetables and fruit were stored in special boxes on deck like this one. Sometimes there was a second box for fresh meat. The two essentials of this type of larder are ample ventilation and insulation. Thick wood was the secret of the insulation. Traditionally, these deck lockers were of varnished teak on expensive craft, and varnished mahogany on less costly boats.

They look delightful and can contain a lot of food, though it is important not to pack in too much otherwise air cannot circulate inside. The lids need clipping down to prevent them being blown open in a gale, and each box needs four short lengths of brass angle-bar, one piece at each corner, with a bronze broad headed bolt to fix the box firmly to the deck.

This type of container relieves the congestion in the galley lockers. It can be used for stowing all sorts of food in waterproof containers but there must be protection from hot sunlight, by an awning or tent over the boom.

LIDS HELD DOWN BY CABIN HOOKS OR HASPS

TOPS, SIDES, AND ENDS OF TEAK OR MAHOGANY ABOUT ¾ INCH~20MM THICK WITH GLUED AND SCREWED JOINTS

LONG VENT SLOT IN CENTRAL BULKHEAD

OPTIONAL DIVIDER MAY BE FIXED OR PORTABLE

TOP HINGES UP FOR ACCESS

T-HINGE BOLTED ON

Ian Nicolson.

BOLT INTO DECK-PLATE

BOTTOM OF ENDS AND SIDES CUT AWAY

VENTILATION LOUVRES OR GRATINGS ON EACH SIDE

HARD-WOOD OR MARINE PLY BOTTOM

VENT HOLES IN BASE I INCH~25MM DIAMETER SPACED 5 INCHES~125MM

SIDE VIEW

SECTION AT A-A

WATER-TIGHT COVER OF P.V.C. OR SIMILAR

FLANGE ON END OF PIPE

AT LEAST TWO TIGHT BANDS OF HEAVY DUTY SHOCK-CORD

CONTENTS TO BE KEPT DRY MAY BE CLOTHES, FOOD, CHARTS, BEDDING, DRY BATTERIES, ETC.

DIAMETER OF PIPE AS AVAILABLE

Ian Nicolson

OVERALL LENGTH TO SUIT STOWAGE SPACE OR AVAILABLE PIPE LENGTHS

A

ROPE HANDLE

A

HOLE FOR ROPE HANDLE

SECTION AT 'A-A'

END PIECE GLUED & SCREWED TO BUNG

SOFT-WOOD BUNG WITH ROUNDED ENDS

COUNTERSUNK 1 INCH ~ 25 M 10 GAUGE SCREWS

FULLY WATER-TIGHT SEALED JOINT

ENLARGED DETAIL

PLASTIC PIPE STOWAGE CONTAINERS

All over the world, it is easy to buy strong plastic piping from builders' merchants. This tubing makes excellent watertight containers when one end has been bunged up, and the other fitted with a watertight cover. These tubes can be used to convey gear safely to a cruiser even when it is raining hard; they keep gear dry even in wet lockers; they can be used to hold emergency equipment for use if the yacht sinks, and are easy to take into a life raft.

A wood end bung is a cheap way of sealing off a tube, but some builders merchants sell flanges which can have ply pads bolted over. Occasionally, it is possible to buy pipe end seals. The end where the gear goes in can be closed off by common plastic bags with ordinary elastic bands, but the arrangement drawn is better. If ordinary plastic bags are used, the first should be put on and sealed with two elastic bands, then the second, and so on.

If these tubes are fixed under the thwarts of a dinghy, they give buoyancy as well as providing dry stowage. Aluminium tubes or fibreglass ones can be used just as well as plastic piping.

PADDED FIDDLES REDUCE BRUISES

Modern boats are light and therefore lively. They jump about and so they throw their crews about. To minimise injuries, there must be no exposed sharp edges and it helps if furniture and other projecting structure is padded.

The padding can be very simple, as shown here. Common foam plastic cushion, bought in strip form or cut from a chunk is glued in place and covered with a suitable cloth. On tough practical no-nonsense craft the covering may be canvas, Terylene or similar material. Often it is the same material which is used to cover the cushions, so it may be a man-made suede, or a leather cloth or one of those tough practical new materials which stand up to so much hard work.

The way the fillet piece under the table top is bevelled so that the joiner can hammer in a row of nails is noteworthy. These nails are totally concealed, and they must be non-ferrous otherwise they will soon rust.

WOOD QUARTER ROUND MOULDING COVERS EDGE OF CLOTH

TOP OF TABLE OR SIDEBOARD OR GALLEY BENCH ETC.

WOOD FIDDLE

LEATHER-CLOTH OR SIMILAR MATERIAL

DENSE FOAM CUSHION STRIP FORMS PADDING

Ian Nicolson

COVERING CLOTH PULLED TIGHT TO ROUND EDGES

FILLET PIECE

FURNITURE FRONT

EDGE OF COVERING CLOTH NAILED AT 1 INCH ~ 25mm CENTRES ALL ROUND ON ACCESSIBLE BEVELLED EDGE

THIS FACE IS INACCESSIBLE TO A HAMMER

GALLEY BENCH OR SIDE-BOARD WORK-TOP

BOLTED ON "SILENT" TYPE CABIN DOOR HOOK
AT EACH END OF EACH FIDDLE

INBOARD FACE VERTICAL

⅛ INCH ~ 3MM RADIUS

FULLY RECESSED HINGES AT
ABOUT 15 INCH ~ 375 ᴹ/ᴹ CENTRES

⅝ INCH
~15MM

Ian Nicolson.

LONGEST POSSIBLE SCREWS

TOP OF LOCKERS OR
UPPER DRAWERS

FIDDLE HEIGHT 2½ INCHES ~ 65MM
MINIMUM AND 4INCHES ~ 100MM
FOR OFFSHORE CONDITIONS

3/16 INCH ~ 4MM BEVEL

1 INCH ~ 25MM THICKNESS FOR 2½ INCH ~ 65 ᴹ/ᴹ HEIGHT
1⅜ INCHES ~ 35MM FOR 4INCHES ~ 100MM HEIGHT

FOLD-AWAY FIDDLE

In a quiet harbour the cook likes to work away at all sorts of interesting concoctions and high fiddles round the galley get in the way. At sea the absence of a full set of sensible fiddles makes cooking impossible in all but the calmest weather. The great attraction of folding fiddles is that they do not get lost during a long spell in harbour, and they are quickly flipped up into position when needed.

The design shown here is held with those strong cabin hooks which do not clink and rattle because they have tapered hook ends which slide into tapered holes in the eyepiece. It is no good securing these hooks with screws because at times the cook will grab a fiddle to prevent being thrown across the cabin, and then the loads on all parts of the fiddle will be serious. Because of these high loadings there must be close spaced hinges held with the longest screws which can be fitted.

Perhaps the only disadvantage of this style of fiddle is that when folded down it prevents locker doors being opened unless their tops are set well below work top level.

FRIDGE FIDDLE

If a fridge, or any similar 'cupboard shaped' container faces athwartships, the contents will fall out when the door is opened on the 'wrong' tack. What is needed is a fiddle on each shelf, but the insides of fridges are not designed to take fiddles. The metal or plastic interior will not easily accept fastenings, and sometimes it is impossible to join anything to the smooth interior lining.

A simple way round the problem is shown in this sketch. Each fiddle is made to jam tightly in place. On one end there is a rubber pad and on the other a tightening device which presses firmly against the fridge side wall. Care is needed otherwise the tightening nut may be turned so hard it will fracture the fridge lining. Once the bolt is pressing its rubber tipped wood nose-piece in place the locking nut is tightened.

This fitting can be used in a dozen different locations, for instance, where there is fine polished furniture which must not be sullied by coarse carpentry.

ENLARGED DETAIL

INSIDE WALL OF FRIDGE

RUBBER OR NEOPRENE PAD

WOOD CHOCK RECESSED FOR BOLT

NON-FERROUS BOLT TYPICALLY ⅜ INCH ~ 10 MM DIAMETER

WOOD FIDDLE

TWO OR THREE ¼ INCH ~ 6 MM DIAMETER COUNTERSUNK BOLTS

NUT WELDED TO LENGTH OF ANGLE-BAR

LOCKING NUT

INSIDE OF FRIDGE PLAN VIEW

WOOD FIDDLE

RUBBER PAD GLUED TO FIDDLE

1 INCH ~ 25 MM
FINGER-GRIP

¾ INCH ~ 20 MM
OR MORE

FIDDLE STANDS
5 INCHES ~ 125MM
ABOVE WORK-TOP

GALLEY WORK-TOP
OR SIDE-BOARD

Ian Nicolson

Z

CUP WASHER

NUT LIGHTLY
WELDED ON

THREE OR MORE ⅜ INCH
10 MM DIAMETER BOLTS

WASHER PLATE

ROUND-HEAD SCREWS
8 OR 10 GAUGE SIZE

VIEW AT Z

FIDDLE FOR OFFSHORE CRUISING

Clear of the protection of land, boats jump about a lot even in moderate weather, and in severe conditions they cavort in every way, though hopefully not to the extent of standing on their head. Working surfaces like galley tops and sideboards need really high fiddles, but no boat, certainly no production boat, has these. This drawing shows a rugged and practical yet easily made fiddle which will be a real asset in deep sea conditions. It will double as a hand-grip provided it is toughly bolted in place, and it is easily and quickly made.

When the time comes to clean the galley thoroughly it will only take a few seconds to remove this fiddle, and in harbour it will be stowed out of the way, beneath a berth or in some similar out-of-the-way location.

The height and thickness of the fiddle will not change much regardless of the size of boat, because the former is dependent on the size of crockery, and the latter on the weight of a man hanging onto it.

The fiddle should be made of a hardwood and the finger-grip should be glued and screwed to the main part, using 1¼in (30mm) 8-gauge screws at 4in (100mm) intervals.

A SEMI-PORTABLE FIDDLE

Fiddles get in the way when the galley is being cleaned or painted, and they are not needed when the boat is in a sheltered berth. It is therefore logical to make them removable, though they must still be strong. The left side of this drawing shows the plan and elevation of a fiddle end fixed to a bulkhead by a pair of vertical slides, so the fiddle drops into place just like a weatherboard. The end of the fiddle which drops in between the slides must be rectangular, to ensure a snug fit.

At intervals along the fiddle there are bolts which can be put in without tools because the heads are knurled, and each nut has a little lever welded to it for hand tightening. The knurled top should have its upper edge well rounded and it should be only about $\frac{1}{4}$in (6mm) thick, so as to be unobtrusive.

END OF FIDDLE KEPT RECTANGULAR TO FIT FIRMLY BETWEEN SUPPORTS

PLAN VIEW

BEGINNING OF FIDDLE TAPER [SEE SECTIONS]

FIDDLE SUPPORTS

BULKHEAD

THROUGH BOLTS WITH KNURLED HEADS

Z

BOLT SPACG 10 INCHES ~250 MM

$\frac{5}{16}$ INCHES 8 MM

Ian Nicolson

BIG WASHER

DOUBLER FOR SCREWS

VIEW AT Z

ROD WELDED TO NUT

7/8 INCH ~ 22 MM OR MORE

ABOUT 5½ INCHES ~ 140MM

Ian Nicolson.

1¼ INCHES ~ 32 MM OR MORE

MINIMUM 1½ INCHES ~ 40ᴹᴹ

¾ INCH ~ 20 MM OR MORE

RECESSED WASHER

VERTICAL SIDE OF FIDDLE

FIDDLE AND FURNITURE SHOULD BE BUSHED WITH TUBING

BUTTERFLY NUT

MINIMUM "BURY" 2 INCHES ~ 50MM

MACHINED SECTION

A SEMI-PERMANENT FIDDLE

Hand slots in fiddles make life easier for the crew, but they must be high and short enough, to prevent cutlery and the like from slipping through. The bottom right sketch shows how the fiddle is secured through the cleating piece which joins the galley (or sideboard) top to its front. Butterfly nuts are shown, but these are not always easy to obtain, which explains why an alternative design is shown on the facing page.

Untapered fiddles look clumsy and unprofessional, but the bevelled side must be away from the work top. The whole of the fiddle is not tapered, a little 'flat' being left at the bottom to make it easy to grip the wood in a vice when working it.

In a boat which is embellished, the fiddle section shown bottom left may be preferred even if it is slightly more difficult to clean.

OFFSHORE BERTH

This design of berth is comfortable when the boat is far offshore in rough weather. It has the added advantages of being light, cheap, easily repaired and it occupies little space athwartships.

As the base is made of cloth, only a thin mattress is needed, and some people have been known to sleep well with no mattress. If a mattress is used it is about one and a half times or even twice the width of the berth base. The height of the inboard leeboard will probably be 15in (375mm) above the berth base, and the battening on the outboard side will extend up roughly the same distance. A sailmaker will make up the base, using something like 10oz Terylene (Dacron) sailcloth and a sewing machine which produces zig-zag stitching. The berth width will usually be of the order of 21in (530mm) wide for the shoulders and hips, and perhaps 13in (330mm) at the foot.

ENLARGED DETAILS

BERTH LEEBOARD

THIN MATTRESS MUCH WIDER THAN BERTH BASE WIDTH

SCREWS AT LEAST 1¼ INCHES ~ 30 MM 12 GAUGE AT 4 INCH ~ 100 MM CENTRES STAGGRD

GLASSED-IN WOOD

CLOTH BERTH BASE

STAGGRD FASTENGS

MATTRESS BETWEEN ½ AND 1 INCH 12 AND 25 MM THICK

PILOT BERTH

HEAVY DUTY CLOTH BERTH BASE WITH TRIPLE ZIG-ZAG STITCHED SEAM UNDER BATTENS

4 INCHES ~ 100 MM CLEARANCE

PARTIAL BULKHEAD

Ian Nicolson

SPECIAL PILLOW MAY BE MADE UP AS PART OF THE ORIGINAL BERTH CUSHION OR ADDED LATER

PILLOW LENGTH 17 INCHES ~ 425 M OR TO SUIT OWNER

HEIGHT 3½ INCHES ~ 85 M OR TO SUIT OWNER

REST OF BERTH MATTRESS IS STANDARD

SIDE VIEW OF BERTH

Ian Nicolson

A

A

WATER-PROOF CUSHN COVER

1 INCH ~ 25 M THICK EXTRA SOFT CUSHIONING

SPARE CLOTHES IN POLYTHENE BAGS

FLAP OVER CLOTHES STOWAGE SPACE

VELCRO SEAL

1 INCH ~ 25 M EXTRA SOFT CUSHIONING

ORDINARY CUSHIONING

PILLOW

MATTRS.

ENLARGED SECTN AT A-A

DUAL PURPOSE PILLOW

The great majority of people like to have a pillow under their heads when sleeping but ordinary 'shore' pillows are not ideal on a cruiser. The one shown here is made as part of the berth mattress, so it cannot slide off the berth. It is covered with the same waterproof material that keeps the mattress dry and easily cleaned.

Instead of filling the pillow with the usual type of wadding, this one has a thin top layer of the softest foam plastic cushioning material. Under it are spare sweaters, shirts and other clothes which are individually wrapped in plastic bags so that they stay dry however much the boat takes in water through the hatches, window leaks, through the ventilators, and so on.

For extra comfort the mattress has an upper layer of the extra soft foam plastic sponge material.

ENGINE ACCESS
AND QUIETNESS

Between a quarter berth and the engine bay it is usual to have a flimsy bulkhead which makes access to the engine hard, but does little to mute the rumble and shriek of the machinery. Instead of a ply panel, a curtain of PVC or similar waterproof material has a lot to recommend it. The curtain is rolled up and secured with three or four tapes while work goes on, servicing or repairing the engine.

The curtain is in two thicknesses with some flexible sound-proofing material between. The noise reducing material is often of foam plastic with a lead insert, so it must be in strips, to allow the curtain to be rolled. Alternatively, the curtain can be a semi-rigid one with a hinge along a line above the sound-proofing.

The stowage pouches are an optional extra likely to be appreciated by the person who sleeps in the quarter berth, as they provide safe, dry stowage in all weathers.

The top of the curtain is held by four or more bolts about 4mm diameter through a hardwood batten in a seam along the top of the material. It is important that the curtain extends far enough to seal gaps between it and the ends of the engine space, and tapes or other securing arrangements will probably be needed here, spaced about every 6 or 10in (150 or 250mm).

COCKPIT SEAT

WOOD BATTEN IN CURTAIN TOP SEAM BOLTED TO COCKPIT SIDE

STOWAGE POUCHES

ENGINE

CURTAIN IN TWO THICKNESSES WITH SOUND-PROOF<u>G</u> BETW<u>N</u>

CURTAIN TUCKS UNDER

SOUND-PROOFED CURTAIN

QUARTER BERTH

VIEW AT A-A

SEE ENLARGED DETAIL

ENLARGED DETAIL

BULKHEAD

A

THIS SECTION OF CURTAIN ROLLS UP FOR ENGINE ACCESS

MATTRESS ON QUARTER BERTH

A

FORWARD

LOOKING TO PORT

Ian Nicolson

ENLARGED DETAIL AT A-A

HALF-BULKHEAD AT HEAD OF QUARTER BERTH

VELCRO

BULKHEAD EDGE PILLAR

WATER-PROOF CURTAIN WRAPS ROUND PILLAR TO KEEP OUT SPRAY

MAIN HATCH

HALF-BULKHEAD

FORWARD

VENTILATOR IN AFT COAMING OF COCKPIT

COCKPIT WELL

VENT SLOTS IN BULKHEAD

AIRFLOW

AIR OVER Q-BERTH

SALOON

A A

Ian Nicolson.

AFT EDGE OF CURTAIN WELL AFT OF HATCH-WAY

BOTTOM OF WATER-PROOF CURTAIN WELL BELOW BERTH

FORWARD EDGE OF CURTAIN WRAPS ROUND BULKHEAD EDGE [SEE DETAIL]

STAYING DRY IN THE QUARTER BERTH

It is hard to stop every drop of water coming in through the main hatch, even with a hood, and even when the hatch is kept shut most of the time. But a wet berth is such a catastrophe that it is worth going to considerable lengths to avoid it.

A good protective curtain is secured tightly along the top, and it extends aft of the hatch, in this case under the bridge deck. The forward end wraps round the partial bulkhead and is held from top to bottom with velcro. The bottom edge does not need securing but it must reach well below the mattress.

With this sort of watertight curtain in place, anyone sleeping in the quarter berth is likely to eventually get a headache from lack of oxygen, which explains the carefully worked in air-flow along the bunk.

AVOIDING BRUISES

The inside of a boat is full of sharp edges which can bruise, even when the boat is in harbour. If padding is fitted round those dangerous projections, the safety and comfort of the craft is enhanced enormously.

The top sketch shows a typical wood, fibreglass or rectangular section metal beam or bulkhead stiffener, or perhaps a mast support pillar. The padding should be as thick as practical and it pays to make up a short experimental section to try in place before fabricating longer lengths. Half inch (12mm) thick foam is abouth the minimum thickness used, but it is hard to get anything as bulky as 1in (25mm) thick to bend round sharp corners.

The middle sketch is a typical angle-bar such as is found in aluminium and steel craft. The bolts through the small flange must be put in first, then the padding is wrapped round and pulled up tight before the final row of bolts is fitted. It is important to have washers under the bolt heads.

At the bottom is a typical furniture or bulkhead edge. Before fitting the padding, the sharp wood edge should be planed away as much as possible. Where possible bolts should be used but if screws have to be put in they must be quite 1in long, so backing pieces of wood may be needed.

Ian Nicolson

CAP NUT

BEAM OR BULKHEAD STIFFENER

ALL SEAMS DOUBLE OR TREBLE STITCHED WITH ROT-PROOF THREAD

BOLTS AT 4 INCH~100MM CENTRES

ROUND OR HEX'G'N̲L̲ HEAD BOLTS ABOUT ¼INCH~6MM DIAMETER

SOFT FOAM PLASTIC

METAL ANGLE BAR

LEATHER-CLOTH OR SIMILAR TOUGH MATERIAL

COUNTER-SUNK BOLTS WITH CUP WASHERS AT ABOUT 3INCH~75M̞M CENTRES

THESE BOLTS MUST BE FITTED FIRST

BULKH̲D̲ OR FURNITURE EDGE

ALL FASTENINGS THROUGH BOTH INNER AND OUTER CLOTH

DOUBLER PIECE FOR SCREWS

COUNTER-SUNK SCREWS WITH CUP WASHERS AT ABOUT 3INCH~75M̞M CENTRES

BULKHEAD COVERED WITH PADDING & DECORATIVE CLOTH

FILLING PIECE COVERS EDGE OF MATERIAL ON BULKHEAD

REBATED DOOR-POST

FLAT STRIP COVERS EDGE OF CLOTH

DOOR LOCK

Ian Nicolson

PLY DOOR EDGE
WELL ROUNDED

HARDWOOD CHOCK IN
WAY OF DOOR HANDLE

SOFT PLASTIC CUSHIONING GLUED TO DOOR

LEATHER-CLOTH OR SIMILAR MATERIAL

PADDED DOORS AND BULKHEADS

It is only in expensively finished boats that padded bulkheads are seen, yet the idea has merit for all sorts of craft. If anyone gets thrown about in rough conditions, it is much better to bump against a semi-soft surface. This type of bulkhead doubling also cuts down noise and helps to insulate cabins. The leather-cloth finish will need regular wiping down in order to keep it clean, but this is more economical than revarnishing or repainting every few years.

This sketch shows how the leather-cloth edging is finished, and how the cloth is never taken round sharp edges. The solid chock in way of the door furniture is important, and a sensible detail is the 'breaking' or planing off of the edges of the solid chock.

A PADDED PILLAR

Those mast support pillars which stand up in the middle of cabins can be bruising in rough weather. Whether the pillar is of wood or metal, it may look ugly and too much like a piece of scaffolding. A smart way to dress it up is to fit it with a jacket made from the same material as the upholstery, or cushion covers, or an attractive leather-cloth . . . or even real leather. If the jacket is padded as shown in the section view, top right, it will be less bruising, and have a pleasant feel, yet will still form a useful handrail.

It will be best to carry the jacket right to the deck head, and down to the cabin sole, but not below it. The jacket can be held in place by a long velcro strip concealed inside a fold-over flat, or by a full length zip, also concealed, or a row of metal fasteners such as are used in dress-making. But, of course, the hooks or press studs must be the non-rusting, heavy duty type.

A pleasant little extra is the row of long narrow pockets for pencils, near the top. After all, pencils are forever getting lost.

ENLARGED SECTION
AT A-A

PADDED JACKET RIGHT ROUND PILLAR

METAL OR WOOD MAST SUPPORT PILLAR

CONCEALED VELCRO OR ZIP

OPTIONAL STOWAGE FOR PENCILS

Ian Nicolson

ELEVATION LOOKING TO PORT

¾ x ¾ INCH ~
20 x 20 M M HARD-WOOD

SLOTS FOR LACING CUT
WITH ELECTRIC JIG-SAW

ENLARGED DETAIL AT 'Z'

SAIL-TRACK WITH
SLIDES ON CURTAIN

WOOD STOP CHOCK
EACH END

Z

CURTAIN EDGE
LACED TO
SCREWED BATN

LACING ⅛ INCH
3 M DIAMTR LINE

BRASS EYES IN
CURTAIN EDGE
FOR LACING

HOOKS HOLD
CURTAIN CLOSED

CURTAIN LOOPS
ON HOOKS

POCKETS FOR
TOOTH-BRUSHES ETC.

OVERLAP 3 INCHES ~
75 MM

GROUND CLEARANCE 1 INCH ~ 25 MM

OVER-LAP 5 INCHES ~
125 MM

A CURTAIN TO AVOID PINCHED FINGERS

A good reason for having a curtain instead of a door is that it cannot pinch fingers or cause other injuries. It gives less privacy, but provided the curtain is thick, perhaps double thickness, and provided it has a good overlap each side, it can be effective.

One way of adding to its effectiveness is to lace one side to a batten which is either drilled with holes all along for the lashing, or scalloped out with a series of cuts, to make it easy to pass the lashing through. Yet another technique is to screw one vertical edge of the curtain to the bulkhead, using round-head screws with larger washers under the heads, or even a thin wood batten. Of course, this is a bit of a nuisance each autumn when the curtain has to be taken away for cleaning.

Using a length of sail track and slides along the top makes sense because ordinary curtain rails are so weak and inclined to rust or corrode.

A TRULY TOUGH DOOR BOLT

Items like hinges, locks and so on are called door 'furniture' in the marine world. They tend to be too weak to stand up to the rigours of life afloat, especially when the sea conditions are very bad, which is, of course, just when total reliability of every component on board is essential.

The owner who wants his locker and door bolts to be beyond reproach can make up this very simple fitting, using an attractive hardwood which matches the rest of the surrounding furniture. If the bolt is fitted inside a toilet compartment, the split pin will be needed to lock the sliding bolt. There will be two holes in the sliding bar, one in the position shown, and the other located so that the sliding bar is secured in the open position.

Screws can be used through the door and bulkhead into the thicker bridge pieces, instead of the bolts shown.

EDGE OF DOOR

EDGE OF BULKHEAD

TYPICAL DIMENSION 3 INCHES ~ 75 MM

SPLIT PIN LOCKS SLIDING BAR

SLIDING BAR SECURES DOOR

SLIDING BAR IN OPEN POSITION

DOOR HANDLE   END STOP

SAFETY LINE   ELEVATION

Ian Nicolson

DECORATIVE HEAD BOLTS

DOOR   OR   BULKHEAD

SLIDING BAR TYPICALLY 1¾ x ½ INCH ~ 45 x 12 MM EDGES WELL ROUNDED

BRIDGE   PIECE

VIEW AT Z-Z

ALL JOINS GLUED & SCREWED

SLOT FOR LATCH

VIEW AT 'A'

BULKHEAD

THIN LINE OR LEATHER

HOLE THROUGH DOOR

LOOP OUTSIDE DOOR FOR LIFTING LATCH

LATCH LIFTS TO OPEN DOOR

SAFETY LINE ON SPLIT PIN

LOCATION OF HOLE THROUGH DOOR WHEN IT OPENS INTO COMPARTMENT

A

PIVOT BOLT

LOCKED NUT

WASHER BETWEEN LATCH AND DOOR

WOOD LATCH

SPLIT PIN PUSHED INTO HOLE LOCKS DOOR

WOOD KNOB

DOOR

BULKHEAD

Ian Nicolson

ELEVATION INSIDE COMPARTMENT

A PRIMITIVE BUT RELIABLE DOOR LOCK

It is a sad fact of life afloat that so few things go on working indefinitely. Even the common door bolt breaks, or the screws get loose, or the bolt is too flimsy to withstand a sudden lurch against the door, or corrosion gives trouble.

The door latch shown here can be made so big and tough that it never fails. And if it needs repairs or modifications the job can be done easily, with only a few common hand tools. The latch consists of a wood bar pivoted at one end, with the other end dropping into a socket. There is a wood knob on the latch to make lifting easy, and tied to this knob is a light line which goes up and through a hole in the door to a loop on the other end. To open the door from the outside, simply pull the loop down. To lock the door on the inside just pop the split pin in the end of the latch to prevent it being lifted.

This simple gadget can be used on doors opening inwards or outwards. In the latter case the latch end must be raised high enough to clear the bulkhead edge. Devices like this give great peace of mind because they are reliable.

A BIG, RELIABLE TURN-BUTTON

So many fittings, especially door and locker components are too small, too flimsy and not able to stand up to the rigours of hard weather offshore. The turn-button shown here can be made easily and it should be indestructible, besides being easy to use with wet, cold hands.

On the locker door there is a wood 'ramp' or wedge, so that as the turn-button is twisted over it, the pressure on the door increases. The small sketch at bottom right shows how the locker door is prevented from being pushed in too far by a rubber door stop. This stop can be packed up simply by adding extra washers, and in this way, wear and tear, warping and distortion, are all taken care off. In this way the door is always held tight and never rattles.

HARD-WOOD
TURN-BUTTON
6 × 2½ × 1 INCH
150 × 60 × 25MM

A

LOCKER
DOOR

LOCKER
DOOR

TURN
BUTTON

B

BOLT ⅜ INCH ~
10ᴹ DIAMETER

METAL PLATE

RAMP OR
WOOD WEDGE

ELEVATION OF LOCKER DOOR

VIEW AT A

RUBBER DOOR-STOP — WASHERS

LOCKER
DOOR

SEMI-SOFT WASHER

LOCKED NUT

VIEW AT B

Ian Nicolson

ENLARGED DETAIL

TAPERED NOSE IN TAPERED HOLE

"SILENT" TYPE CABIN HOOK HOLDS DOOR SHUT

PLAN VIEW

ENGINE CASING

GALLEY FRONT OR SIMILAR

HOOK HOLDS DOOR OPEN

'SILENT' TYPE HOOK

For all sorts of jobs like holding ladders up or down, and doors closed, there is nothing to beat the simple cabin hook. But it must be the 'silent' type, because otherwise the fit of the hook into the eye is slightly sloppy, and the grip of the hook less than perfect.

A 'silent' hook never rattles, and unless the boat turns upside down it will not release its hold. It is ideal for such jobs as holding an engine casing door shut, because the same hook can engage in a second eye, to hold the door open when there is work to do on the engine.

CATCHES AND CLIPS

The top sketches show a type of metal retaining catch which is used to hold up covers and lids which have horizontal hinge lines. These include chart table tops, which hinge up to allow charts to be taken out of the locker below, ice-box and freezer lids, folding seats and so on. To prevent the lid banging back and forward between the bulkhead and the rotating plate when the boat rolls or pitches, the lid handle has a rubber knob on top and the handle almost fills the space for the lid. The rubber knob can be a door stop.

At the bottom of the drawing is a simple 'pendulum' plate which pivots on a bolt. Where it is absolutely impossible to fit a bolt, a long, strong screw is used. The plate is normally bronze, brass or stainless steel though thick perspex may be used. It is a help to the crew if the contents of the drawer or locker are marked on the plate, even if the words have to be shortened. When the boat is in harbour, the plate is rotated anti-clockwise till it lies on top of the stop screw, and this lets the drawer or locker open unhindered.

LID CATCH

PIVOTING PLATE

VIEW AT 'A'

EDGES TURNED 45°

BULKHEAD — DOUBLER
BASE-PLATE
TUBE
LID HANDLE
RUBBER STOP
SECTION
ICE-BOX LID OR SIMILAR IN OPEN POSITION

CATCH IN "HARBOUR" POSITION

STOP SCREW

FL'RES ROKTS

BOLT
NUT AND LOCKING NUT
PIVOTED METAL PLATE

FRONT ELEVATION

SECTION

LOCKER DOOR OR DRAWER FRONT

SAFETY CATCH FOR LOCKERS & DRAWERS

BOLT WITH CAP NUT ACTS AS
STOP ON PIVOT PLATE

LOCKED CAP NUT

PLAN VIEW

BOLT WITH HEAD CUT OFF
WELDED TO ANGLE-BAR

SHORT LENGTH
OF ANGLE-BAR

PIVOT PLATE TILTS OVER TO
ALLOW LID TO FOLD DOWN

SHORT LENGTH OF METAL SECT'N

ELEVATION

STAGGERED
FASTENINGS

ICE-BOX LID OR CHART-TABLE
TOP OR OTHER HINGE-UP
COVER IN RAISED POSITION

RUBBER DOOR-STOP OR SIMILAR PAD

BULKHEAD OR FURNITURE FRONT OR SIMILAR

A LID CLIP

There are so many places on boats where a catch or retaining clip is needed to hold up a hinged cover, lid, or folding top. Typical examples are ice-boxes which have top access, those chart tables which lift, hinge-up engine casings, and cabin tables which hinge up to stow against a saloon bulkhead.

This neat, pivoted catch suits all these and many more situations. The one shown here is so simple that it can be made by an amateur with few tools to hand. A professional would probably machine a slot in the top flange of the angle-bar and have the pivoted catch in the slot, to give a symmetrial appearance. And he would use a length of rod tapered each end with a ground-away weld as a pivot. The gadget shown here can be made to any size, to suit any weight of door or lid, and it should be proof against the worst conditions.

LOCKER DOOR STAYS

That thin brass chain which is used to pull the traditional type of lavatory cistern is ideal for preventing locker doors opening too far. A retaining chain is needed each side unless the locker door is under 10in (250mm) wide.

To prevent the chains catching between the door and the locker front when the door is shut, the chains are angled in, and at the top they have chocks which ensure the whole chain is well in from the door sides.

Where possible, the chain end should be held by a bolt. Where this cannot be arranged, the end screw should be long, as thick as possible, and have a washer under the head to prevent the chain coming off.

CHOCK HOLDS CHAIN AWAY FROM LOCKER SIDE

LONG STRONG ROUND-HEAD SCREW WITH WASHER

LIGHT BRASS CHAIN

BOTTOM OF CHAIN HELD BY BOLT SET WELL IN FROM LOCKER DOOR SIDE

FIDDLES MAKE FOLDED DOWN DOOR INTO A TEMPORARY SHELF

CHAINS NEEDED BOTH SIDES OF LID

FIDDLE 3 INCHES 75ᴹᴹ OR MORE

RECESSED HINGES

LOOKING INTO LOCKER

Ian Nicolson

LOCKER BOTTOM

SETTEE SEAT BACK

SECTION THRO' LOCKER

BULKHEAD DOUBLER

BULKHEAD

LADDER CORNER MUST BE ROUNDED

STAINLESS STEEL OR BRONZE CHANNEL BAR ABOUT 4 INCHES ~ 100mm LONG

LOCKED BOLT MATCHES CHANNEL BAR

ELEVATION OF DETAIL

WASHER

GLUED WOOD DOUBLER STIFFENS LADDER SIDE AND FILLS WIDTH OF CHANNEL BAR

PLAN VIEW OF DETAIL

Ian Nicolson

STAGGERED 3/16 INCH ~ 5mm BOLTS

HOOK OR EYE, ON ONE OR BOTH SIDES FOR ROPE

LADDER SWINGS UP FOR ACCESS TO ENGINE ETC.

HOLE FOR SUPPORT ROPE

EASILY MOVED CABIN STEPS

Nothing is so awkward as heavy cabin steps which have to be shifted to get at the engine, or lockers, or maybe the main fuse board. If the steps are portable they cannot be pushed negligently forward into the cabin or they will damage the furniture and crew as the boat plunges about.

The arrangement shown here has the advantage that no one in the cockpit will try to come down the steps when they have been moved. Also, it is a fairly effortless job to lift the bottom of even heavy steps. The rope used to support the steps may be lashed to a hook or eye which also supports the leeboard of a berth.

At the bottom of the steps there must be recessed wood chocks to keep the sides exactly in place. The top is hinged by pivot bolts through short lengths of channel bar, and this metal section should be bought before making the steps. Though full length steps are shown here, this technique can be used for shorter steps extending from an engine casing down to the cabin sole.

SLOPED STEPS FOR SAILING CRAFT

When a yacht is heeled, the cabin steps are tilted and dangerous. By having the steps angled up each side life is made safer for the crew. For added strength the angled part of each tread may be continued down under the horizontal part, as shown here.

The top of the engine casing normally has no bevelled top area, but this is illogical, and the arrangement shown on the right makes a lot of sense. On the left, the usual type of fiddle is shown, though this important safety feature is often omitted or made flimsy and incapable of standing up to a heavy foot crashing down on it. It should be quite $3/4$in (20mm) thick.

Though these steps are shown on the front of an engine casing, they can be fixed to a bulkhead or some other structure. They must be strongly secured with glue and at least three 12-gauge screws for each of the three parts of each step. An advantage of this design is that the side and centre portions form a triangle, strengthening each other.

CABIN ENTRANCE

MAIN PART OF STEP 9 INCHES ~ 230 MM OR MORE IN WIDTH

HEAVY DUTY FIDDLE 3 INCHES ~ 75MM HIGH

ALTERNATIVES

UNUSUAL BUT LOGICAL CASING TOP SHAPE

MINIMUM WIDTH 5 INCHES ~ 125 MM

NON-SKID SURFACES

ENGINE CASING

STEPS $3/4$ INCH 20 MM THICK

ENDS DO NOT MEET TO SIMPLIFY CONST'ION

TILT ANGLE ABOUT 25°

STEP WIDTH 7 INCHES ~ 175 MM OR MORE

Z

Ian Nicolson

LOOKING AFT

VIEW AT Z

$1/4$ INCH 6 MM

END TAPERED

SPINNAKER POLE END FITTINGS

←— COCKPIT —→

Z ←—

←— ALLOY TUBE HAND-RAIL

FORWARD —→

←— CABIN STEPS ARE PORTABLE FOR FRONT ACCESS TO ENGINE

HANDRAIL ACROSS CABIN ENTRANCE FOR SAFETY

VIEW AT ARROW Z
WITH STEPS REMOVED

ENGINE SPACE DOOR OPEN

HANDRAIL & SAFETY RAIL

It is common practice to have cabin steps which have to be taken away in order to gain access to the boat's engine. When the steps have been removed, someone may not notice and step into the cabin with painful results. To prevent this type of accident, a handrail which can be swung across the cabin entrance is easy to make.

At the aft end of the handrail there is a pivot, and at the fore end a clip which engages in a metal eye. The clip and eye can be a set of spinnaker boom inner end fittings, and the same arrangement may be used at the aft end of the handrail. Indeed, the whole fitting may double as a spinnaker bearing-out spar, used to prevent the spinnaker sheet cutting into the windward shrouds and getting so far inboard that the sheet winch cannot haul the boom aft.

Though the handrail in the top sketch is shown to be horizontal, it can run down parallel with the steps. If there is an aft cabin, the same type of swing-across handrail can be used there too.

EACH FOREHATCH STEP IS A BOX

If there are no steps to a forehatch it can be hard work climbing up, perhaps using a berth leeboard as one foothold, and maybe a locker door top as another. The steps shown here can be made at home, away from the boat, and secured in convenient places such as on a bulkhead, with one possibly on a berth front, and the top one on the inside of a cabin coaming, if it is vertical and the hatch edge is close.

Each step doubles as a small stowage locker with an open front. The sides of the mini-locker are carried up to form fiddles so that when the boat is heeled or is rolling, a foot on the step will not slide off.

The bolts securing each step must be in line with the locker opening, otherwise drilling and counter-sinking the bolt holes will be difficult if not impossible.

BULKHEAD

DOUBLER PIECE GLUED ON STIFFENS BULKHEAD

FIDDLES PREVENT FEET SLIPPING OFF STEP

STEP AT LEAST 5 INCHES 140 MM WIDE

ABOUT 3 INCHES ~ 75 M

A

A

DISTANCE BETWEEN STEPS ABOUT 12 INCHES ~ 300 M.M.

EACH STEP FORMS A SMALL STOWAGE BOX

SECTION AT A-A

HANDGRIP 4½ INCHES ~ 115 M.M. OR MORE IN WIDTH

Ian Nicolson

FIDDLE KEEPS GEAR IN LOCKER & FORMS HAND-GRIP

FIDDLE ROUGHLY 2 INCHES ~ 50.MM HIGH

ENLARGED DETAIL

HOLES FOR TWO 5/16 INCH ~ 8mm STAINLESS STEEL
BOLTS WHICH KEEP LADDER IN PLACE

1/4 INCH ~ 6MM ALUMINIUM PLATE
FORMS HOOK OF BOAT-HOOK

SEE ENLARGED DETAIL

WELDS 2 INCHES
50 MM LONG

FORWARD
HATCH

TWO BOLTS HOLD
LADDER TOP

3 INCHES
75 MM
OR MORE

STEPS OF 3/8 INCH
10 MM THICK ROD

TUBE ABOUT 2 INCHES
50 MM DIAMETER

END OF TUBE PLUGGED

STEPS ABOUT 16 INCHES ~ 400 MM APART

Ian Nicolson

CHOCK WITH HOLE FOR BOTTOM
OF LADDER BOLTED TO CABIN SOLE

FORWARD CABIN LOOKING TOWARDS BOW

FOREHATCH LADDER & EMERGENCY BOAT HOOK TOO

This forehatch ladder is light in weight, simple, and it takes up very little space. It is also easy to remove during the winter refit. For a boat which is permanently in a marina, and therefore seldom has any need for a boat hook, this ladder has a second use: it can, with just a little delay be converted into the latter. For a blue-water cruiser it has the advantage of being a reserve boat hook because these items of deck gear are more often lost overboard than worn out.

If the ladder is never to be used as a boat hook, it can be heavier and made out of steel. There should never be just one bolt at the top, and if the ladder is to be taken down in a hurry the nuts should either be of the butterfly type, or have lengths of rod welded to them so that they can be taken off without using tools.

SIDE LADDER

Nothing looks smarter than a well-varnished hardwood side ladder, especially if the top hooks are of polished bronze. It used to be possible to buy special hooks which had double straps, one for the inside and one for the outside of each side piece of the ladder. Nowadays, it is usually necessary to make up the top hooks. The ones in this drawing are of $1 \times \frac{1}{4}$in (25×6mm) metal flat bar, recessed into the wood side piece. Instead of bending the metal straps over at the top, hardwood chocks are fitted and as these lodge on the toe rail there is no risk that a wood or aluminium toe rail will be damaged.

A side ladder need not extend below the waterline but if it does there is less chance a dinghy will get under it and lift it off; besides, if anyone goes bathing, or falls overboard, a ladder extending a foot (300mm) below the water makes it much easier to get back aboard.

1 INCH ~ 25 MM

AT LEAST 9 INCHES 225 MM

AT LEAST 6 INCHES 150 MM

SECTION AT A-A

SAFETY LINE EACH SIDE OF ¼ INCH~6 M M ø ROPE

1½ INCH ~ 40 M M HARD-WOOD CHOCK BETW.ᴺ MET.ᴸ STRAPS

TOERAIL

Ian Nicolson

HAND-HOLD SLOTS AT LEAST 6×2¼ INCHES 150 × 55 MM.

STEPS ABOUT 11 INCHES 275 MM APART

AT LEAST ONE ¼ INCH 6 M M BOLT AND TWO 12 GAUGE SCREWS ALL COUNTERSUNK

AT LEAST TWO SOFT PADS EACH 8 INCHES~ 200 MM LONG

BOTTOM TWO STEPS ARE FOR GETTING OUT OF THE WATER

A   A

EDGES OF TREADS AND
ALL OF SIDES VARNISHED

—PADDING

—STAGGERED
SCREWS

WOOD LEFT BARE
FOR A GOOD GRIP

AT LEAST $\frac{3}{5}$THS
TREAD WIDTH

PLAN VIEW

LADDER TREAD

Z   Z

SIDES USUALLY 1 INCH ~ 25 MM THICK
AND SELDOM LESS THAN ¾ INCH~20MM

—LADDER SIDE

—STEP SLOTTED
THROUGH

Ian Nicolsan

PROFESSIONAL TECHNIQUE

—EXCESS CUT OFF
AFTER GLUE HAS
FULLY HARDENED

ALTERNATIVE

SECTIONS AT Z Z

ALL JOINS
EPOXY GLUED

AMATEUR TECHNIQUE

SCREWS HIDDEN FROM VIEW

—FILLET PIECE
1×1 INCH ~ 25×25 M
M

SIDE LADDER

The best side ladders are made from teak and glued up using epoxy resin. The area to be glued must be degreased, as the wood contains natural oils.

The steps can be morticed right through the sides as shown in the middle drawing, but not every amateur feels confident he can cut a neat, tight mortice. Admittedly, with modern epoxy glues and their fillers a tight join is not essential, but for some amateurs the join shown at the bottom will be more popular. The fillet pieces are screwed and glued to the side pieces first. When the glue has set, the treads are screwed and glued in place. By locating the screws as shown, they will seldom be seen.

At the top of the top drawing the padding is shown. By keeping its fastenings on the sides of the ladder sides, there is no chance of scratching the topsides.

Anyone who wants a very light ladder can enlarge the hand slots in the sides and cut 1in (25mm) slots in the treads. In any case, all edges should be well rounded.

PROPS AND LADDER FOR BOATS LAID UP

This type of boat support is not cheap, especially when compared with the simple under-hull wooden shores made from lengths of untrimmed fir trees. On the other hand it does have a lot of advantages. It cannot come away from the boat by accident, even if the boat is being buffeted by hurricane force winds. It cannot be kicked away from under the boat by mistake or by vandals. It does not need moving when the underside is being anti-fouled, and it can be used to carry a concealed electric cable up to a light for scaring burglars as well as to a handy board for plug sockets.

Perhaps the biggest asset is the set of steps, which obviates the need to have a ladder. Admittedly, it is not easy to climb these sorts of steps, especially when carrying gear.

The tube should be about 1^1/$_2$in (35mm) in diameter for every 10ft (3m) of boat length. It is best to have the steps extending up well above deck level, so that they act as hand holds.

CLEAT FOR TACKLE END

TACKLE MAY BE PART OF YACHT'S RUNG RIGG

VIEW AT A ENLARGED

JUNCTION BOX FOR ELECTRIC POWER POINTS

MASSIVE PADDING

LIGHT FOR NIGHT WORK AND DISCOURAGING BURGLARS

CHAIN PLATE

STEPS OF ^{3}/$_8$ INCH ~ 10 ROD OR ^{3}/$_4$ INCH ~ 20^M TUBE

BOAT SUPPORT PILLAR

AMPLE ORDINARY PROPS AS WELL

ELECTRIC CABLE BURIED IN TRENCH

BASE-PLATE SIDES 9 INCHES ~ 225^M LONG FOR EVERY 20 FOOT ~ 6 METRES OF BOAT'S LENGTH AND LARGER ON SOFT GROUND

END OF COCKPIT WELL

HARD-WOOD PAD

RECESSED CHOCK

LOCKING-IN PIN

BOLT RIGHT THROUGH OR DROP-NOSE PIN OR ROD WITH END EYE AS SHOWN

A

FOOT-REST IS AN ALUMINIUM SCAFFOLD POLE OR SIMILAR

CLEAT FOR SAFETY LINE

FOUR 3/16 INCH ~ 5MM BOLTS

ENLARGED DETAIL

VIEW LOOKING ATHWARTSHIPS

CLEAT FOR SAFETY LINE ON LOCKING-IN PIN OR DROP-NOSE PIN

VIEW AT A

LOOKING FORW? OR AFT

SEE ENLARGED DETAIL

SECTION THRO' COCKPIT

LOOKING FORW? OR AFT

CHOCKS AT DIFFERENT HEIGHTS TO SUIT VARIOUS LEG LENGTHS

FOOT-REST SUPPORTED AT EACH END BY RECESSED WOOD CHOCKS

COCKPIT FOOT-REST

There is nothing so uncomfortable as sitting in a boat which is heeling, and not being able to put both feet on a secure resting place. The adjustable bar, extending fore-and-aft through the well of the cockpit is a well-known fitting, though it is not liked by everyone because when tacking there is a chance someone will fall over it. But we cannot always cater for the heavy-footed people, and in time they learn to avoid these obstructions. In any case, for a series of short tacks the foot-rest can be removed and stowed out of the way.

There should be at least two, and perhaps as many as four different sets of chocks, to cater for very small and very large people. A single, vertical hardwood backing pad can be used with a succession of slotted thick chocks to take each tube end. If a short rod of stainless steel, perhaps made from a bolt with the head drilled and the thread ground away, is used to hold the tube in place, it should have a safety line secured tightly to its cleat to prevent it coming out.

AVOIDING SORE BACKS

When sitting outboard in a typical modern sailing yacht, the helmsman and crew find they are leaning against the lifelines. As these are normally thin wires, even tough, experienced crew object to the discomfort and the helmsman finds it hard to concentrate if his back is being 'sawn in half'.

A well-tried way of improving the cockpit comfort is to fit lengths of webbing instead of lifeline wires. Toe-strap webbing can be bought from chandlers or from sailmakers. The latter will work eyes in each end, as shown at the top, but amateurs armed with nothing but some strong sail twine, a needle and palm and a little patience can stitch their own loops onto the webbing. If no metal eye is used, the webbing must be inspected monthly for chafe.

An end lashing or a rigging screw is essential to keep the webbing tight. Owners who are worried about windage, fold the tape edge to edge, and stitch it together before putting the end eyes in place. A back-up wire which may be of thin gauge should run outboard of the webbing: this is compulsory under RORC safety rules.

FOUR FULL TURNS OF 3/16 INCH~4 MM DIAMETER TERYLENE~DACRON

HYDRAULICALLY PRESSED METAL EYE OR HAND SEWN RING AND TURN-OVER

PROFESSIONAL WORK BY SAIL-MAKER

DOUBLED OVER

HEAVY DUTY ZIG-ZAG STITCHING

AMATEUR STITCHING

2 INCH~50 M WIDE HEAVY DUTY WEBBING

DOUBLE THREAD MULTIPLE CROSS-STITCHING ALL ROUND

ENLARGED DETAILS

CREW CAN LEAN BACK IN COMFORT ON BOTH RAILS

ONE END SHACKLED ONE END LASHED

PULPIT OR DIAGLY STRUTD STANCHN

Ian Nicol

16 INCHES
400 MM

½ INCH ~ 12 mm MARINE PLY

ENLARGED DETAIL

SECTION AT A-A

¾ INCH ~ 20 mm

1¼ INCHES ~ 30 mm

1½ INCHES ~ 40 mm

ALL JOINS GLUED AND SCREWED

3 INCHES
75 MM

VIEW AT B

SLOTS 12 × 4 INCH
300 × 100

B

A

A

COCKPIT WELL

COCKPIT SEAT

FOOT-REST COMBINED WITH LADDER

This helmsman's foot-rest can also be used as a ladder, either over the yacht's side, or up to a high quay. It is made from marine ply so that it is strong and will last. On each side, glued and screwed flanges of wood cover the ply edges and make the whole unit rigid. At each end are knee-shaped chocks which keep the foot-rest at the right height above the seats.

All edges must be well rounded and the whole fabrication should have four coats of varnish, or even more. People with large feet, and hence even larger seaboots may prefer larger slots than those shown, and a good case can be made for assembling a rough mock-up or template of the whole unit, before starting to cut the wood.

ADJUSTABLE FOOT-REST

When a boat is heeled the helmsman needs a comfortable stance if he is to steer a good course and enjoy his job. Above all, he needs a foot-rest which he can adjust to his own height, and maybe change after an hour or two, to relax his muscles. He also needs a foot-rest which suits different angles of heel.

This foot-rest consists of two vertical pieces of wood shaped to suit the cockpit seats, and held together at each end by top and bottom wood straps extending fore-and-aft. Inside each piece of wood there is a length of track. Two alternatives are shown here in the enlarged details at the top. On the left is a section of genoa sheet lead track with a tube about $^3/_4$in (20mm) in diameter welded to each carriage on the two tracks. The plungers on the carriages locate the foot-rest bar.

The alternative, shown on the right, is an ordinary sail track with slides made up of either a steel T-bar section cut and filed to size or alternatively a special short length of section welded up from steel flat bar. Wood cross-pieces take the helmsman's feet and the carriages are fixed along the tracks by split pins or bolts through the tracks.

ALTERNATIVE SECTIONS AT 'A-A' MUCH ENLARGED

NON-SLIP SURFACE GLUED ON

ALUMINIUM SAIL TRACK

¾ INCH
20MM

12 GAUGE SCREWS
IN BATCHES OF FOUR

STEEL T-BAR SECTION

GENOA SHEET LEAD TYPE
OF TRACK AND CARRIAGE

TUBING WELDED TO CARRIAGE

ALL JOINS GLUED AND SCREWED

LIGHTENING HOLES

ENLARGED DETAIL
SECTⁿ AT B-B

A

B

A

B

COCKPIT SEAT

COCKPIT WELL

COCKPIT TO SUIT THE TALL AND THE SHORT

SEE ENLARGED DETAIL

ENLARGED DETAIL

— ROUND-HEAD SCREWS STAG^RD

— SEMI-SOFT AND METAL WASHERS

SECTION AT 'A-A'

└ COCKPIT WIDTH-REDUCER

WIDTH-REDUCER TAPERED IN PLAN VIEW

A

— COCKPIT WELL →

18 INCHES ~ 450 MM

26 INCHES ~ 650 MM

A

— COCKPIT SEAT →

└ MAIN HATCH

Ian Nicolson

COCKPIT COAMING ┘

Because people are not all the same height, they do not all favour the same width of cockpit well. What everyone does want is a bench which has the opposite seat edge just the right distance away for resting the feet on, when the boat is heeling.

The plan view shows a cockpit well which was originally too wide. It has been narrowed by a pair of tapering strakes of hardwood, so that it is narrow at the aft end and wider forward.

In practice, the tiller may obtrude, and also these ideal widths may be impossible to achieve without absurdly wide strakes. However, this sketch shows what to aim for. If in doubt, it is best to make the cockpit well slightly narrow, because the crew can always sit with knees well bent.

IDEAS FROM LANDAMORE'S OYSTER

Leslie Landamore built a 43-footer (13m) Oyster type with this elegant helmsman's seat. It is shaped so that the helmsman sits level even when the yacht heels, a very desirable asset if the boat is steered with a wheel.

Under the ends of the seat there are lockers for gas cylinders, but because the seat is slatted, the lockers are difficult to detect, and this reduces the chances of the gas cylinders being stolen. Each locker lid needs a shockcord downhaul to prevent it flipping open in windy conditions, and, of course, a lock is needed.

The gas lockers drain into the cockpit, and the gas would accumulate in the well if the cockpit drains discharge below the waterline. The cockpit drains must also run downhill all the way otherwise water will accumulate in the pipes and gas will not be able to escape. To save frequent swopping of gas bottles, they can be linked to the cooker in pairs or even in threes. However, when the boat is left for a period, or if there is to be no cooking for a day, all the bottles should be shut off, to eliminate any chance of leakages.

1½ INCHES ~ 40MM

GAPS ¼ INCH ~ 6MM

½ INCH ~ 12MM

SCREWS 1¼ INCH ~ 30MM 8 GAUGE BRASS

1 INCH 25MM

HARD-WOOD ~ NOT PLY-WOOD

SECTN AT A-A

SEE ENLARGED DETAIL

TWO GAS BOTTLES LINKED TOGETHER TO SUPPLY COOKER

HELMSMAN'S SEAT SUITS ANGLES OF HEEL

PART OF SEAT FORM LOCKER LID

SHOCK-CORD

LOCKER FOR SPARE CYLINDERS

COCKPIT WELL

CALOR GAS LO'KRS DRAIN INTO C'PIT

BULKHEAD SHOWN CUT AWAY TO REVEAL INSIDE OF GAS LOCKER

COCKPIT DRAINS MUST BE PERMANENTLY ABOVE W'TR-LINE

VIEW LOOKING AFT

LOWER TUBES ~ NOT WIRES ON PULPIT FOR EXTRA SECURITY

5-LEG PULPIT IS STRONGER & MORE RIGID THAN 3-LEG TYPE

HIGH TOERAIL KEEPS OUT SPRAY AND GIVES EXTRA SECURITY

FORWARD COCKPIT LID SHOWN DOTTED

HEADSAIL CUT HIGH FOR SAFETY & VISIBILTY UNDER

LARGE DEEP COCKPIT FOR SAFETY & COMFORT

LARGE ROLLER FOR ANCHOR CHAIN SET LOW DOWN

AFT FACING SCOOPS WITH EXTRA LARGE DRAINS AND NON-RETURN VALVES

STEM-HEAD BOLTS EASILY CHECKED

LARGE DRAIN THROUGH STEM

SUNKEN, SNUG AND SAFE

When building a new boat or changing an old one, there are a dozen arguments in favour of fitting a deep capacious forward pit. Working in it – sitting, standing or kneeling – the crew are far less likely to fall overboard than if up on deck. They can wedge themselves in, and should have some extra protection from wind and waves especially if the toe-rail is extra high.

Such a capacious pit must be well drained, hence the two aft and single bow outlets. Any two of these should be capable of emptying the pit in a couple of minutes, and in any case even a full pit should never be so big that it can contain enough weight of water to endanger the vessel. The bottom of the pit must be strong enough to support a full load of sea.

The bow roller is designed so that it is easy to use. Being lower and larger than usual the crew have a less muscle-aching time heaving the anchor chain onto it, and over it.

When the foot of the headsail is higher than the pulpit there will not only be a much better view forward and fewer bashed heads, but also the chafe on the sail will be reduced.

ANCHOR LOCKER IMPROVEMENTS

The fibreglass lids on many anchor lockers are slippery and none too strong. Both defects can be cured simultaneously by fixing hardwood strips on top. Teak is best but costly; afrormosia is tough and some people find it acceptable unvarnished. The tread strips should be fixed with close-spaced and well-staggered screws driven up from below. They form ridges which enable the crew to wedge their feet along the edge when the deck tilts.

The inside of the locker is an ideal place to have a stowage pouch for sail tiers, and others for deck tools like a knife, a pair of pliers for jambed snap shackles, and a shackle spanner to open ordinary shackles. The inside of the locker may be padded with PVC or a similar cloth to prevent the ground tackle from damaging the fibreglass of the locker.

DOUBLY ENLARGED DETAIL

AT LEAST ⅛ INCH ~ 3MM

TREAD-STRIP

SEMI-SOFT WASHᴿ

ROUND-HEAD SCREWS SPACED 3 INCHES ~ 75 MM

WASHERS AND SCREWS OF STAINLESS STEEL

LID OF FIBREGLASS

ENLARGED DETAIL

SECTION AT A-A

BETWEEN 1½ & 3 INCHES ~ 40 & 80 MM

BETWEEN ½ & ⅞ INCHES ~ 12 & 20 MM

POUCH FOR SAIL TIERS

SHOCK CORD ALONG TOᴾ

ABOUT 1/30ᵀᴴ BOAT'S LENGTH

HARD-WOOD TREAD-STRIP WITH ROUNDED ENDS

KNIFE PLIERS & SHACKLE SPANNER IN POUCHES

DEPTH ABOUT HALF THE LENGᵀᴴ

SECTION THROUGH COCKPIT
LOCKER LID INBOARD EDGE

— COCKPIT LOCKER LID

— SMALL SIZE RUBBER DOOR-STOP.
TWO UNDER EACH LID

— THIS EDGE TENDS TO BANG
DOWN AND GET CHIPPED

— COCKPIT WELL SIDE

PLANE OFF
WOOD CHOCK TO
CORRECT HEIGHT

AT LEAST THREE SCREWS WELL STAGGERED

LOCKER LID HANDLE OF
TERYLENE OR NYLON WEBBING

AT LEAST TWO AND BETTER
STILL FOUR 3/16 INCH~5 M BOLTS

RUBBER OR
NEOPRENE PAD

Z

RUBBER OR
NEOPRENE PAD

SECTN THRO'
LOCKR LID EDGE

VIEW AT Z

NOISE DEADENERS

For anyone trying to sleep below, activity in the cockpit can be infuriating. In particular, if anyone bangs down a cockpit locker lid, the crack can waken even exhausted foredeck hands. The top right sketch shows how common domestic door stops may be used to prevent lids banging down. The exact height of the rubber stop is critical and is adjusted by planing away the top of the wood chock, before fitting the rubber knob.

Some lids can be quietened by putting simple rubber discs on the surface where the lid thumps down, but these may not stay in place for long. The bottom pair of sketches shows a rubber noise checker which is bolted in place so that when it wears out it is easy to replace, and until that time it will stay where it is put. The webbing handle has the virtue that it will cause no bruises.

BRUISE REDUCER

There is nothing so disconcerting as being bashed on the head by a boom. The gadget shown here minimizes damage in two ways:

1 The bright orange cover of the padding warns everyone in the firing line of the danger, and as it swings towards them, they have a chance to duck out of the way.

2 Even if the boom does make contact with someone's head, the ample padding changes a nasty thump into a more muted shove.

The padding may be of the same soft foam used in boat cushions, or the closed cell type which is made into lifejackets. The latter does not soak up rain, as the cushion type will. These pads may be made up by anyone with a tough sewing machine, or by a local sailmaker.

When screwing the padding onto a boom, the fastenings near the end should be very close together, and all fastenings must be set on top of the boom clear of the padding which covers the area likely to bang into a crew member.

FASTENINGS ARE 6 GAUGE STAINLESS STEEL SELF-TAPPING SCREWS AT 2½ INCH~60 MM CENTRES

DOUBLE ROWS OF ZIG-ZAG STITCHING DONE ON A SAIL-MAKER'S MACHINE

FORWARD

BRIGHT ORANGE COVERING OF HEAVY DUTY P.V.C. MATERIAL

AFT END OF TAPERED BOOM

CLOSED CELL FOAM PLASTIC

TOPPING LIFT CLEAR OF BOOM END

OUTHAUL

REEF PENNANT

SLIT FOR PENNANT

Ian Nicolson

PADDING AT LEAST ¾ INCH~ 20 MM THICK PER 30 FOOT~ 9 METRES OF BOAT LENGTH

PADDING ALWAYS CARRIED RIGHT ROUND AFT END OF BOOM

CHEEK BLOCK FOR REEF PENNANT UNDER PADDING

AFT END OF UNTAPED BOOM

ROPE TIDY BAGS

Ropes in the cockpit tend to get snarled together. When the weather is bad the crew may not have time to coil up those halyards and reefing lines which are led aft, or there may be seasickness aboard, so no one has the inclination to take sensible precautions.

Bags keep ropes separate, tidy and ready to run out quickly. Terylene (Dacron) or PVC or a similar tough cloth is used to make light, long-lasting bags. Each one should hold only one coil, and each bag should be slightly too large for its coil. Before ordering the bags from a local sailmaker, each coil should be measured to get the correct size. As a rough guide a 40ft (12m) coil of $\frac{1}{2}$in (12mm) diameter rope needs a bag quite 18in (450mm) deep and 10in (250mm) across.

Sometimes a length of shockcord is fitted inside the top outer seam to keep the bag closed.

WOOD, METAL, OR PLASTIC ANTI-CHAFE STRIPS ON AFT EDGE OF CABIN TOP

WOOD OR FIBREGLASS BATTEN IN TOP [AND BOTTOM] SEAMS OF BAG

BOLTS SPACED ABOUT 5 INCHES ~ 125 MM

DOUBLE-STITCHED SEAMS

ENLARGED DETAIL AT 'A-A'

CAP NUT

P.V.C. OR HEAVY SAIL-CLOTH

SEMI-HARD & METAL WASHERS

WINCH

JAM CLEATS

A

A

TOP OF BAGS AT LEAST 3 INCHES ~ 75 MM BELOW CABIN TOP DECK EDGE

DRAINS AT CORNERS

VIEW LOOKING FORWD FROM COCKPT

HALLIARD & REEFG LINE BAGS

Ian Nicolson

BAGS FOR MAIN SHEET, SAIL TIERS ETC.

COCKPIT WELL FRONT

THREE-LEGGED MAST PULPIT OR GRANNY RAIL

For working at the bottom of the mast in anything but the quietest weather, there is nothing so helpful as a pulpit, sometimes called a 'granny rail'. This rather unkind expression disguises the fact that without the rail, work takes longer, people fall overboard more often, halyards are lost aloft more frequently, and beginners are sometimes put off sailing.

The pulpit feet must be very strongly bolted down with at least three $^1/_4$in (6mm) bolts in each flange. If the under-deck chocks are recessed for the nuts, there is less chance of a bloody scalp for tall crew members.

The legs may be fitted with $^1/_4$in (6mm) diagonal stiffening bars at the top to make the whole fitting more rigid, and if two people are to use the pulpit in severe conditions, a four-legged pulpit would be better. Whatever kind is fitted, it is usual to use stainless steel for the fabrication, but galvanised steel is often far cheaper, and as strong.

ENLARGED DETAILS — TOP CHOCK IS SMALLER THAN LOWER ONE

BASE FLANGE $^1/_4$ INCH~6MM THICK

1 INCH~25 MM TUBING

$^1/_2$ INCH 12 MM

ROUNDED EDGES

CABIN TOP DECK

PLAN VIEW

MAST

ABOUT 16 INCHES~400MM

$^3/_8$ INCH~22 MM

HARD-WOOD CHOCK WITH BEVELLED EDGE

NUTS RECESSED INTO CHOC PREVENT INJURY

SEE ENLARGED DETAIL

MAST

THREE-LEGGED MAST PULPIT OR 'GRANNY-RAIL'

ABOUT 30 INCHES~750 MM

OPTIONAL STIFFENER

Ian Nicolson

ELEVATION LOOKING TO PORT

OUTER TUBE ROTATES TO CLOSE AIR INLET SLOT

INNER TUBE DUCTS AIR TO FORWARD AND AFT LEGS

DIAGONAL SUPPORT LEG

AIR INLET

SECTⁿ AT A-A
ENLARGED

MAST

AFT LEG OF 'GRANNY RAIL' VENTILATES SALOON

TOP TUBES ANGLED DOWN FOR DRAINAGE

FORWARD LEG OF 'GRANNY RAIL' VENTILATES FO'C'SLE

ABOUT 3FT 6INCHES 1·050 METRES

AIR INLETS

FORWARD

Ian Nicolson

DIAGONAL LEG EXTENDS OUTWARDS
LOOKING TO PORT

BASE FLANGES BOLTED TO CABIN TOP DECK

GRANNY RAILS WHICH ARE ALSO VENTS

Those rails, a bit like pulpits, which are located port and starboard of a mast, to hold the crew in position when halyards are being handled, or reefs put in, are often called 'granny rails'. They have to be high to be effective, and must be well bolted down if they are to survive harsh offshore conditions.

There is no reason why they should not double as ventilators, and being so high they should be acting in clear air, almost always above spray level. Even if spray does drive in, the slope of the top tubes should ensure that water will flow back out of the inlet hole. When the going gets too rough the air inlet is sealed by rotating the outer tube, shown in the enlarged detail at top right. This outer tube must be kept well lubricated otherwise it may corrode onto the inner tube.

It is essential to have the outboard diagonal support tube otherwise the crew, when leaning against the rails, will soon weaken the base flange fixings of the main tubes. This fitting can be made of stainless steel or, to save money, of mild steel fully galvanised after the welds have been ground smooth and the base flange holes drilled.

WIND SOCK VENTILATOR

In hot climates, there is no more popular ventilator than the wind sock, because it channels masses of cooling air into the boat through the fore hatch. These socks are made from spinnaker nylon because this is a hard wearing material which stows away in a small space. It is also 'wind tight' so there is no loss of airflow through the pores, and it is widely available.

It is also soft and pliable which means anyone can simply push aside the trunking of nylon cloth in the hatchway and climb in or out quite easily. The mouth of the sock must be kept open, and sail batten material is as convenient as anything for this. Some sailmakers just sew a length of fibreglass battening into the seam of the mouth, while others add a vertical or horizontal batten to hold the mouth in an oval shape, as shown here.

HALLIARD FIXED TO SHACKLE ROUND FORE-STAY

WIND-SOCK FORWARD ROPE TIED TO SHACKLE

WIND-SOCK AFT GUY

FORE-STAY

SHACKLE ROUND F-STAY

DOWN-HAUL TIED TO CLEAT ON FORE-DECK

WIND-SOCK MADE OF SPINNAKER NYLON

SIDE GUYS TIED TO GUARD-RAILS

AIR IN

AIR FLOW

Ian Nicolson

FRONT VIEW OF WIND-SOCK MOUTH

TUBE OF WIND-SOCK SAME SIZE AS FORE-HATCH

BATTEN[S] IN SEAM ROUND MOUTH

BATTEN KEEPS MOUTH OVAL

TWO STEPS AT SAME LEVEL
FORM MASTHEAD PLATFORM

TOP STEPS MAY BE 4 FEET~
1.200M BELOW SHEAVES OR
MASTHEAD INSTRUMENTS

WHEN WORKING ALOFT
A SAFETY HARNESS MUST
ALWAYS BE WORN

$\angle \frac{3}{16}$ INCH~4MM LINE
KNOTTED AT EACH STEP

LINE PREVENTS HALYARDS
FROM CATCHING ON STEPS

STEPS MUST BE HELD BY
AT LEAST 5 RIVETS EACH

LINE MUST BE TIGHT

IF A RIVET GETS LOOSE
IT MUST BE REPLACED

STEP SPACING
14 INCHES~350MM FOR
SMALL PEOPLE
20 INCHES~ 500 MM
FOR GIANTS

REDUCE STEP SEPARATION
BY 1INCH~25MM FOR EACH
1½ INCH~40MM MAST WIDTH
OVER 8 INCHES~200MM

Ian Nicolson.

MAST STEPS

For long range cruising, a set of steps up the mast may not be essential, but they do take a lot of the worry out of sailing. They make it so much more comfortable for the person going aloft. Even if he is in a bosun's chair, he will be able to steady himself all the way up, and he can take some of the load off the halyard.

The height of the steps depends on the owner's choice; he may feel that a jambed or unrove halyard is the most likely problem aloft, in which case he will have the steps located to deal with these problems. Alternatively, he may worry more about his mast-head instruments, in which case he will arrange to have the steps fitted higher, to make working on the gadgetry easy.

Steps need a light line made fast all the way down, port and starboard, to prevent halyards from tangling with the steps.

NO TROUBLE ON THE FOREDECK WITH HEADSAILS

In strong winds, some headsails are hard to get down. A downhaul rove through extra large eyelets at every other jib hank, or maybe every third or fourth, makes the job easy. If the sail fights hard the downhaul can be taken to a winch on or near the mast.

During prolonged gales, headsail hanks sometimes wear through, and, even more often, come adrift. To avoid subsequent trouble when the sail is being lowered in a ferocious breeze, the eye on the halyard should have a shackle through it and round the forestay, so that the head of the sail is held close to the forestay. This shackle, if permanently used, also reduces the chance of the halyard being lost aloft. Even when it does get adrift, it is easier to recapture if it is shackled to the forestay.

By fitting another shackle to the tack pennant and round the forestay, a headsail is further kept under control when being hoisted or lowered in tough conditions. Also, the halyard end can more easily be clipped onto the pennant when not in use.

SEE ENLARGED DETAIL

FORESTAY

HEADSAIL HALLIARD

STAINLESS STEEL SHACKLE WITH LOOSE TUBE ON PIN

STRONG SNAP SHACKLE

HEAD OF GENOA

ENLARGED DETAIL

DOWNHAUL THREADED THROUGH EXTRA LARGE JIB HANK EYELETS

SEE ENLARGED DETAIL

FORESTAY

SHACKLE AS ABOVE

TURNING BLOCK FOR DOWNHAUL

FOOT OF SAIL

STRONG SNAP SHACKLE

HEADSAIL TACK PENNANT

ENLARGED DETAIL

NORMAL SPINNAKER BOOM LIFT

SPINNAKER BOOM. IT MAY HAVE EXTENSION PIECE FOR LONGER REACH

ANCHOR LIFTING LINE HAS SNAP-SHACKLE FOR CLIPPING ON ANCHOR

LEAD BLOCKS EACH END OF SPINNAKER BOOM

WINCH ON MAST

TWO GUYS HOLD BOOM STEADY

HEAVY ANCHOR

CHAIN OR WARP SLACKENED OFF ONCE ANCHOR LIFTING LINE IS CLIPPED ON

ANCHOR HANDLING

To take the hard work out of lifting a heavy anchor on board, rig the spinnaker pole complete with its usual topping lift. A pair of light ropes steady the outer end of the pole, and an anchor lifting line is led from a mast winch via two turning blocks to the anchor. The boom is used like a derrick, and the halyard winches provide the power to lift the heavy weight. To bring the anchor inboard, once it has been hauled to the surface, the anchor lifting line is clipped on. The chain is now either disconnected, or slackened away, and the anchor hoisted to the boom end. The boom is swung aft a little, then topped up, and so the anchor is positioned over its chocks on deck. Lowering the anchor exactly where it is needed is easy enough as the lifting line is gently surged round the winch. The whole job can be done single-handed, slowly, stage by stage.

TRIP STOPPER

Any obstruction on deck can be dangerous as well as hurtful, if the crew are inclined to trip over it. Those stainless steel tracks for the genoa sheet lead blocks are all too prone to stub toes, especially during a dark, wet night.

If tapered strips of wood are fixed along each side of the tracks, the foot is guided over the obstruction, and the track can be walked over quite comfortably. At each end of each track there must be a tapered chock to match the side strips. When this sort of end chock is fitted, the usual plastic end stops which prevent the track cars from coming off accidentally are not needed.

This drawing shows another gadget: the short length of plastic tube (or non-ferrous spring) round the shackle which holds the sheet lead block. The tube prevents the block from falling over and banging on deck. In light airs, when a sail is filling and collapsing, the constant chatter of a block on the deck will keep the watch below wide awake, which is maddening.

HEADSAIL SHEET LEAD BLOCK

ELEVATION

EDGE TAPERS TO ⅛ INCH ~ 3 MM

PLASTIC PIPE OR NON-FERROUS SPRING KEEPS BLOCK OFF DECK

DECK

SHEET LEAD TRACK

HARDWOOD STRIPS PREVENT ACCIDENTS

PLAN VIEW OF TRACK END

DRAIN-WAY

END CHOCK

Ian Nicolson.

A

A

SECTION AT A-A

"LADDER" TYPE TILLER EXTENSION FOR THE BEST GRIP

LONGER TILLER GIVES EXTRA LEVERAGE

Ian Nicolson.

PIVOT LINE IS CENTRE-LINE OF STOCK

ADDITIONAL RUDDER AREA ON FORWARD EDGE

A A

AREA FORWARD OF STOCK CENTRE LESS THAN 1/6 TOTAL AREA

ORIGINAL RUDDER BLADE

LAYERS OF FIBREGLASS CHOPPED STRAND MAT AND WOVEN CLOTH

WOOD ADDITION TO FORWARD EDGE WELL FAIRED OFF

ENLARGED DETAIL AT 'A-A'

REDUCING WEATHER HELM

The discomfort of a tugging tiller can be reduced by applying various techniques, even if the heavy weather helm cannot be fully eliminated.

The most obvious trick is to make the tiller extra long, so that the work needed to hold it to windward is less. Just as important, the tiller extension should be of the ladder type which is easier to grasp for long periods, not the straight tube type which is used on dinghies.

Another technique is to increase the rudder area forward of the pivot line. This needs doing with caution, and as a general rule the total area forward of the centre of the stock should never exceed one sixth of the total area. Naval architects often advise that the area is increased progressively (on the leading edge), as shown in the enlarged detail.

TILLER LOCK

There are various types of lock for holding the tiller in a particular position. Some consist of a form of ratchet, with a tongue on the bottom of the tiller which engages in the ratchet; some are in the form of a wood plank athwartships under the tiller with holes in to take pegs, one peg going each side of the tiller. These locks are not entirely satisfactory because the spacing of the ratchet troughs, or the holes in the plank for the pegs, may not suit the required tiller location precisely.

The arrangement shown here is infinitely variable allowing the helmsman to set the tiller just where he wants it to achieve self-steering, or make the boat heave-to.

The type and size of jam cleat will depend on the size of rope and boat. The rope size shown will suit boats up to about 40ft (12m). Each rope should have a knot in it so that the helm cannot be put over more than 35 degrees. This is the limit for effective steering, because beyond that angle waterflow breaks down and steering becomes less effective. Going astern with more than 35 degrees of helm can cause damage to a rudder.

PLAN VIEW

U-BOLT WHICH MAY DOUBLE AS FIXING POINT FOR PERSONAL LIFE-LINE

COCKPIT WELL

ROPES 5/16 INCH 8MM DIAMETER

TILLER

A

COCKPIT COAMING

DOUBLER CHOCK GLUED TO UNDER SIDE OF TILLER

JAM CLEAT AND FAIRLEAD

VIEW LOOKING TO PORT

KNOT

TILLER

ALTERNATIVES

ENLARGED DETAIL AT 'A'

DOUBLERS

PLAN VIEW

WING OR BUTTERFLY NUTS ARE TIGHTENED BY HAND

SLOTTED METAL PLATE ALLOWS EXTENSION ANGLE TO BE ADJUSTED QUICKLY

SECTION AT A-A

SLOTTED PLATE

ENLARGED DETAIL

BOLTS ⅜ INCH ~ 10 MM DIAMETER

TILLER EXTENSION

FORWARD END OF TILLER

PLAN VIEW OF COCKPIT

EXTENSION FORWARD END HINGES UP FROM HERE

TILLER AT NORMAL WEATHER HELM ANGLE

HELMSMAN SITS ON CABIN STEPS AND LOOKS OUT OFTEN!

COCKPIT WELL

Ian Nicolson

COMPASS ON CHART TABLE

EXTENSION IN MIDDLE OF BOAT

MAIN HATCH

SAILING IN THE DRY

This trick works well with old, steady yachts, but for very 'flighty' craft which will not hold their course even for a few seconds, it may be hard to operate. The helmsman sits in the warmth and comfort of the cabin and steers a course by compass. The hand-bearing compass, if big and steady enough, can be mounted on the chart table, or the main compass may be one of the semi-portable type with more than one mounting bracket. Care is needed to ensure there is no steel near the compass which will affect it.

The fore end of the tiller extension should pass through the cabin entrance at the middle, when the tiller is in the normal 'weather helm position' if the boat is going to windward or reaching. Just occasionally, the helmsman may need to make a big movement of the extension and so he will have to hinge its forward end up to clear the door posts of the cabin entrance.

To steer below decks takes practice and skill but in time it is possible to cook with one hand and steer with the other.

COCKPIT PROTECTION

Quite a few yachts, especially motor-sailers, are having windscreens fitted at the fore end of the cockpit. It can be a costly exercise, but if the window components are standard, or are made rectangular, or at least with two opposite sides parallel, the total expense can be limited.

It is almost always best to set the windscreen forward of the bulkhead at the fore end of the cockpit, and secure wood 'grounds' across the cabin top deck. The tops of these wood sections are straight, while the bottom faces follow the curve of the decking. Through bolts or ample screws driven upwards hold the grounds in place, as shown in the bottom detail.

The top enlarged section shows one good way of making the top edge strong and safe. The padding reduces the chance of injury, and if there is a cockpit hood this can be made watertight at the forward end by pulling it down tight onto the padding.

LEATHER-CLOTH COVERING ON SOFT PADDING

CLOSE SPACED ROUND-HEAD SCREWS

STANDARD METAL WINDOW FRAME

TOUGHENED GLASS WINDSCREEN

WOOD CAPPING HAS RECT^{LR} SECTION

ENLARGED SECTION AT A-A

FORWARD

WINDSCREEN

Ian Nicolson

CABIN TOP DECK

PERSPEX CANNOT BE USED HERE IF THERE IS A WINDSCREEN WIPER

METAL WINDOW FRAME

WOOD SECTION BEVELLED OFF

AMPLE BEDDING NEEDED AT ALL JOINTS

CABIN TOP DECK

STAGGERED SCREWS SPACED ABOUT 3 INCHES ~ 75 MM

ENLARGED DETAIL

SEMI-SOFT RUBBER MOULDING

FIXED LOWER PART OF WIND-SCREEN

GLASS EDGE ROUNDED

WATER-TIGHT HINGE

OVERLAP
2 INCHES ~ 50mm
OR MORE

HINGED TOP
OF WINDSCREEN

SIGHT LINE

SEE ENLARGED DETAIL

Ian Nicolson

HELMSMAN'S
PLATFORM

COCKPIT OR WHEELHOUSE

TYPICALLY 3 INCHES ~ 75MM
HELMSMAN'S PLATFORM

CHOCK FOLDS UNDER
TO REDUCE HEIGHT

ENLARGED DETAIL

A BETTER VIEW, ESPECIALLY IN THICK WEATHER

Nothing makes a boat so comfortable as an enclosed, or partly enclosed steering position. However, in foggy or rainy conditions the windscreen becomes covered over with moisture, and it can be hard to see forward. A marvellous invention is the divided window which has a top half hinged at the top. In foggy weather the upper part of the window is opened and the view much improved. If the fog turns to rain the window is lowered till the helmsman just has a thin slit to look through, but no rain gets in, and not much draught either.

Naturally, the height of the helmsman's eye is critical, as it must be just above the top of the bottom part of the window, so that there is a good view over the sealing strip, shown in the enlarged detail (top right). At the bottom right the detail shows a simple way of making the helmsman's platform vary in height. There can be two folding chocks (at the front, and back naturally), instead of the single folding one sketched, to give more height variations.

A BREAKWATER FOR DRYNESS

Water pouring aft along a deck finds its way through hatch edges, into ventilators and generally works its way below. A good way to keep the aft deck and inside of a boat drier, is to have a breakwater, or even two, on the foredeck.

A breakwater must be strong and it often needs metal support brackets if the height is over about 8in (200mm). And if it is too high to step over easily, it needs one or two doorways through. The brackets are usually bolted to the deck and the breakwater, and are typically 3ft (1m) apart. They should extend to the end of the breakwater which must reach to the deck edge for full effectiveness.

It is important that the breakwater looks smart since it stands out so boldly. The wood used must match the rest of the deck trim if the final finish is varnish, as it usually is. All edges must be very well rounded, and the bottom edge must be bedded in a semi-soft waterproof compound.

BREAKWATER — ALLOW AMPLE WORKING SPACE SUCH AS 30 INCHES ~ 750 MM BETWEEN WINCH & BREAKWATER — ANCHOR WINCH

ELEVAT.ⁿ

OUT TO DECK EDGE — GATEWAY NEEDED FOR BREAKWATER MORE THAN 18 INCHES ~ 450 MM HIGH — GATEWAYS MAY BE FITTED BOTH SIDES

PLAN VIEW

RAKE ANGLE USUALLY BETWEEN 20° AND 40°

STIFFENER — FILLET — DECK

SECT.ⁿ AT A-A ENLARGED DETAIL

HEAVY GAUGE CLOSE SPACED SCREWS OR BOLTS — DOUBLER

BOLTS AT 4 INCH
300M CENTRES

WELDED OR FLANGED

AMPLE BEDDING

DECK

METAL COAMING

GLUED AND SCR'W'D JOINS

WOOD COAMING

SEE ENLARGED DETAILS

WATER-PROOF COVER PULLED TIGHT ALL ROUND

HIGH COAMING FORWARD

DECK

Ian Nicolson

ELEVATION

CHAIN HOLE TOO INACCESSIBLE FOR A PLUG

FORWARD

BREAKWATER ROUND WINCH PROTECTS CH⁰ HOLE

PLAN VIEW

CHAIN HOLE UNDER GIPSEY

NO WATER DOWN THE CHAIN HOLE

A persistent trickle of water through the anchor chain hole when offshore is common on a wide variety of craft. It is surprisingly difficult to stop rain and spray getting into the hull through this access because the hole is usually awkwardly hidden under parts of the anchor winch.

To get round the problem, a breakwater is fitted right round the winch. It is made as high as is reasonably convenient, especially forward where the waves come tumbling aboard. A tightly fitted cover goes over the top of the breakwater. This protects the winch from the weather and stops rain dribbling below. To make the cover fit snugly there must be a double lip on the top of the breakwater, and the lashing in the seam round the cover must be at least $1/4$in (6mm) thick so that it can be pulled really tight.

WATERTIGHT CHAIN PIPE

Pipes through foredecks for anchor chains seldom have good covers. Some have metal lids with slots which fit over one link of the chain, but in rough weather this lets in bucketfuls of water every hour. What is needed is a device which excludes all water even if the boat goes upside down.

This simple device is made by taking a chock of a hardwood like teak, mahogany or iroko, and turning it or whittling it to fit the chain pipe. The plug must taper slightly so that it can be jammed in place, and at first it must be made a little too large. Next, it is sawn vertically and the exposed faces chipped away till the chain lies fairly snugly between the two halves. The plug is now glued together. The hole where the chain passes through is blocked at the bottom with plasticine, plastic wood or even a stopping compound, and epoxy resin is poured down the hole at the top. This binds the chain and the plug together and ensures permanent watertightness.

PLUG CUT IN HALF AND CARVED TO FIT CHAIN — EPOXY GLUE FILLS GAPS

HALVES EPOXY GLUED TOGETHER WITH CHAIN IN MIDDLE

SECTION AT A-A

LIGHTLY TAP PLUG TO MAKE PIPE WATER-TIGHT

JERK CHAIN UP TO FREE PLUG

HARD-WOOD PLUG TURNED OR CARVED

CHAIN SHACKLED TO ANCHOR

CHAIN PIPE WITH NO COVER

DECK PAD

Ian Nicolson

DECK

RING OR SQUARE PLATE WASHER

CHAIN FALLS DOWN TO ITS LOCKER

DOUBLER TAPERED OUT BEYOND DECK PAD TO AVOID HARD SPOT

TURN-BUTTONS EACH END OF HINGED-UP WOOD COVER

PLAN VIEW

HINGE

THIS PART HINGES UP

ELECTRIC CABLES TAPED TOGETHER

DECK

WOOD CHOCK BOLTED DOWN

WOOD CHOCK BOLTED DOWN

ELECTRIC JUNCT'N BOX

Ian Nicol

METAL OR PLASTIC PLATE WITH A COUNTER-SUNK HOLE FOR EACH ELECTRIC CABLE

BEDDING

SECTION VIEW

ELECTRIC CABLES THROUGH THE DECK

Down the mast there are often several cables which have to be led through the deck. On some boats the wires are taken to so-called waterproof plugs which tend to leak. On other craft the cables pass through glands which seldom keep the water out after two or three years' use.

This multiple gland is ingenious because it can be made to take any number of cables, and it is also cheap and simple to fabricate from easily available materials. It will stand up to heavy feet and heavy weather and if it is of varnished teak it will be very smart.

The outer two strips of wood are bolted down, and the middle one is hinged. Before it is shut down, all the cables are passed through their holes, then lots of soft bedding is squeezed around the wires where they go through the metal or plastic plate. When the lid is shut down, this forces the bedding tight round each cable, and the two (or more) turn-buttons keep the lid tight.

DRIP PROOF MAIN HATCH

Most main hatches let water in at the slides, and at the forward end. This design is in the form of an up-turned tray, and when shut the rubber seal along each side and across the front is bedded down tight on the coamings which stand up from the cabin top deck.

To open the hatch, the aft end is lifted enough for the aft turned-down lip to clear the side coamings, then the whole hatch is pushed forward. It is hinged to a sliding unit which glides forward along two tracks which are set closer together than the hatch sides.

Each part of the hatch is easily made and simple to repair. It can be fitted on a wide variety of boats, the top can have a big window in it, and the design permits any level of massiveness or lightness, according to whether the boat is for long-range cruising or inshore racing.

HANDLE ON OUTSIDE

HANDLE ON INSIDE

HATCH CLOSED   FORWARD

HATCH THREE QUARTERS OPEN

SLIDE END STOP

TWIN SLIDES

TOP WEATHER BOARD WITH SEAL STRIP ON TOP

SEE ENLARGED DETAIL

SECOND WEATHER BOARD

TOP OF HATCH

CABIN TOP DECK

DRIP THROWER

HINGE

SLIDING UNIT

RUBBER SEALS GLUED INSIDE HATCH LID

Ian Nicolson

SLIDES PORT & STARB⁰

SLIDE END STOP

OUTBOARD

SECTION AT 'A-A'

ENLARGED DETAILS

E FLANGE 4 INCHES ~ 100$\overset{M}{M}$ WIDE WELL BEDDED ALL ROUND

'S $\frac{5}{16}$ INCH ~ 8$\overset{M}{M}$ DIAM$\overset{TR}{}$ AT 2½ INCHES ~ 60$\overset{M}{M}$ CENTRES

NSLUCENT PLASTIC $\frac{3}{8}$ INCH ~ 10$\overset{M}{M}$ THICK

ROD OR TUBE EDGING ALL ROUND LID

BAFFLE WITH MINIMUM CLEARANCE

HATCH OF $\frac{1}{8}$ INCH ~ 3$\overset{M}{M}$ THICK STEEL OR ALUMINIUM ALLOY

HINGE WELDED OR BOLTED

2 INCH ~ 50$\overset{M}{M}$ WIDE SOFT RUBBER SEAL GLUED ALL ROUND INSIDE HATCH TOP

½ INCH ~ 12$\overset{M}{M}$ DIAM$\overset{TR}{}$ ROD OR TUBE FULLY WELDED ALL ROUND TOP OF COAMING

BOLTS $\frac{5}{16}$ INCH ~ 8$\overset{M}{M}$ DIAM$\overset{TR}{}$ AT 2½ INCH ~ 60$\overset{M}{M}$ CENTRES

DECK DOUBLER ALL ROUND HATCH OPENING TO COMPENSATE FOR LOST STRENGTH. EDGES ROUNDED

DECK MAY BE OF ANY MATERIAL

TOTALLY WATERTIGHT LOW COST HATCH

This simple hatch can be made of aluminium or steel by any amateur or professional metal worker for very little money. The size will be made to suit the space on deck, the requirements of the crew (who may want to pass large sailbags through), and the structure of the boat.

The hatch height too can be adjusted to suit circumstances. If it is on the main weather deck and the boat is to go far offshore it will be best to have coamings 8in (200mm) high or even more. But if it is on a cabin top, and the boat is a sleek one with no serious projections, then the coamings may be 2in (50mm) high or even less.

If the hatch is of steel, the top and lower parts can be galvanised before being joined at the hinges. In addition, or instead of galvanising, the steel may be coated with epoxy paint.

The hasp and bolts or clips fitted will depend on what is available or what can most easily be made up.

Watertightness is ensured by the wide, soft rubber strip which is compressed on the coaming top. This is so much better than the narrow rubber used on so many commercial hatches because the latter lack ample width of glued surface and the rubber sometimes works clear of the metal edge.

WATER BARRIERS ON A SLIDING HATCH

Driving spray filters in around the edges of sliding hatches unless precautions are taken. Shown here are some of the barriers, seals and baffles which can be fitted to many types of sliding hatch. On the left is a simple wood lip hinged onto the aft flange of the hatch top. When the hatch is closed, the lip folds down and shuts off that narrow gap above the top weatherboard.

To stop water driving in under the forward end of the hatch, there is the usual box or 'garage' over, but this is far from watertight. It can be made tighter by fitting a rubber sealing piece under the aft edge of the cover, designed to press down constantly on the hatch top. As a second line of defence there is that vertical seal bolted to the forward flange of the hatch top, and a third line of resistance is the semi-soft seal which doubles as a bumper and stops the hatch banging into the vertical flange at the aft end of the cabin top deck. Just for good measure there is another similar seal above. Naturally, it is not always possible or necessary to have all these seals on one boat.

RECESSED HINGE BOLTED TO WOOD LIP

AFT END OF HATCH COVER OR 'GARAGE'

RUBBER SEAL PRESSES DOWN ON TOP OF SLIDING HATCH

AFT END OF HATCH TOP

WEDGE FORCES RUBBER SEAL DOWN

Ian Nicolson

CABIN TOP DECK

RUBBER SEAL PRESSE DOWN ON CABIN TO

SEMI-SOFT SEAL FORMS BUMPE

SEMI-SOFT SEAL

TOP OF UPPER WEATHER BOARD

SEAL GLUED AND SCREWED INSIDE LIP

LIP HINGES UP TO ALLOW HATCH TO SLIDE FORWARD

VIEW LOOKING TO PORT — FORWARD →

MAIN HATCH

ALM-ALLOY ⅛ INCH~
3MM THICK

STAINLESS STEEL BOLTS
5/16 INCH~8ᴹ DIAMETER
SPACED 4 INCHES~100ᴹ

ENLARGED DETAIL

AMPLE BEDDING

HARDWOOD

CAP NUTS

CENTRE-LINE

SEE ENLARGED
DETAIL

HANDRAIL

A

VIEW LOOKING AFT
AT ARROW 'A'

Ian Nicolson

ELEVATION —FORWARD

MAIN HATCH PROTECTION

The usual waterproof cloth hood over a main hatch needs renewing every few years. Also, it is not strong, and in very severe conditions it may be swept away. The one shown here is much tougher, being made from aluminium alloy plate. It has thick plastic windows bolted at 2in (50mm) intervals all round, so that the joins round the window edges form thick bands of stiffening. More reinforcing is provided by the handrails and the flange round the aft edge which is in the form of a gutter on edge. This prevents water flowing aft and under the cover.

This sort of hatch hood can be made semi-permanent, so that it is left off the boat when she is gently weekending inshore. Then, when she goes far from home, into deep waters, the hood is bolted in place. It would suit a boat which, for instance, does a limited number of rough races each year, and perhaps one long cruise. For these events she would have the hood bolted in position, but for the rest of the time it would be left at home in the yacht's store.

LEAK-FREE SLIDING HATCH

Not only is this hatch unusually well guarded against water seepage, it is also low in profile. For a racing boat where the crew want to be able to walk unimpeded over the hatch, this type is almost as good as one which is entirely flush with the deck. The latter type is likely to be expensive and in practice less than completely watertight.

The top section shows how the hatch sides and aft end are tightly clamped down, forcing the perspex top to lodge right down on the slides. In practice, the perspex may wear too fast if the hatch is often used, so mating strips of metal would, in this case, be secured on the underside of the perspex to run on the slides. Alternatively, metal or a suitable hard-wearing plastic can be used instead of perspex.

The bottom sketches show how the fore end of the cover is supported and water prevented from driving in. These details can be built into other designs of hatch.

DECK OR CABIN TOP DECK — LOCKED CAP NUT
FULL LENGTH METAL SECTION — SLIDE — STIFFENER ALONG FULL LENGTH OF HATCH
PERSPEX HATCH TOP
SEMI-SOFT WASHER
METAL WASHER
BREAKWATER
METAL WEDGE UNDER CLAMP PAW
CLAMPS AT AFT END OF HATCH PORT, STARBOARD, & ON CENTRE-LINE

VIEW LOOKING FORWARD OR AFT

BREAKWATER FORMS END STOP AND SUPPORT FOR FORW.D PART OF HATCH TOP
BREAKWATER ACROSS FRONT
FORE END OF PERSPEX HATCH TOP IN CLOSED POSITION
STIFFENER
FORWARD
Ian Nicolson
DECK
NEOPRENE SEAL ACROSS HATCH FRONT
HATCHWAY EDGE TRIM

HATCH FULLY OPEN   HATCH CLOSED

VIEWS LOOKING ATHWARTSHIPS

HANDLE RIGHT ACROSS
ACTS AS WAVE DEFLECTOR

FILLET MOULD^G WELL BEDDED

HINGES BOLTED ON

FULL WIDTH PERSPEX TOP WITH ROUNDED EDGES

LARGE DRAIN-HOLES
ALL ROUND

STAGGERED SCREWS

DRAIN-WAY ALL
ROUND HATCH

SECT^N A-A & B-B

PLAN VIEW

FORWARD

NON-SLIP STRIPS
WITH 3 INCH ~ 75 MM
GAPS BETWEEN

Ian Nicolson.

A   B

A   B

SIDE ELEVATION

DOUBLE-COAMING HATCH

WOOD FOREHATCH WITH IMPROVEMENTS

This hatch is a traditional design with improvements. Water which seeps in between the cover and the outer coaming drains out again via the drain holes. These are $5/8$in (15mm) diameter or more so that they do not get bunged up with debris.

All round outside at the bottom, there is a fillet moulding, but this is only an extra line of defence because those upward driven screws, zig-zagged at 3in (75mm) intervals not only secure the hatch to the deck tightly but also keep out leaks.

By having the perspex right to the edge of the hatch there is less maintenance, and the traditional type of edge moulding is eliminated. This again reduces chances of leaks in future years, when the hatch is beginning to weather. Non-slip strips have to be close together so that there is no chance of a shoe getting between them, and so skidding.

A wood handle extends right across the aft edge and deflects solid water from the top of the outer coaming. This coaming, as well as the inner one and the filler piece between are all the same thickness and are glued together.

CHANGING A FOREHATCH

The top sketch shows typical defects in an inefficient hatch. Water can easily run in under the outer flange and the rubber seal is either right away from the upstanding flange or not compressed tightly enough, or the rubber seal may be discontinuous, or it may have perished. Often the cheapest way of getting a watertight hatch is to buy a standard Lewmar or similar hatch and bolt it down over the deck opening.

It is normally necessary to build up some form of coaming to take the new hatch and in the main sketch here, a wood coaming and underdeck doubler is shown. However, for anybody who prefers to work in fibreglass or metal, the new base for the hatch can be in these materials.

Whatever form the new hatch base takes, there must be very good seals wherever water is going to try to penetrate. The cost of the bedding compound is nothing compared with the discomfort of just one leak. This is why a hatch must be bolted, never screwed down. The bolts must be tightened progressively in the same way as an engine cylinder head is tightened, to avoid distortion. First of all, the nuts are wound up finger-tight, then the forward starboard one is slightly tightened with a spanner followed by the aft port one, then aft starboard, then forward port. Next, the intermediate bolts are gently spannered in the same order. Finally, all the nuts are pulled hard up in the same order.

CABIN TOP DECK OR MAIN DECK

GAP TOO LARGE

THIN WEAK COVER

RUBBER SEAL DOES NOT TOUCH RIM

BAD OUT-DATED HATCH

TRANSPARENT COVER

STRONG RIGID FRAMEWORK

SHARP METAL RIM BITES INTO RUBBER SEAL ALL ROUND

SCREWS THROUGH OLD COAMING INTO NEW WOOD ON

UNDER-DECK DOUBLER

WOOD TRIM COVERS BOLT ENDS

COPIOUS BEDDING

MODERN WATERTIGHT HATCH

WATER BARRIER KEEPS MOST WATER AWAY FROM SEAL

RUBBER SEAL ⅝ × ¼ INCH ~ 16 × 6 MM
THICK ENSURES WATER-TIGHTNESS

⅜ INCH ~ 16 MM
MARINE PLY

STIFFENER I × ⅝ INCH ~
25 × 16 MM GLUED

STRAP HINGES WITH
STAGGERED SCREWS

FOUR BUTTERFLY NUTS
PULL HATCH DOWN TIGHT

ANGLE-BAR SCREWED
TO COAMING

PACKING PIECES
MATCH COAMINGS

COAMING ¾ INCH ~ 20 MM

HISTORICAL HATCH

Myth of Malham, designed by Laurent Giles, had probably more influence on offshore sailing than any other yacht. This sketch shows her forehatch, which like every other component on board was carefully planned to do its job well.

The long-tailed hinges with wide spread fastenings ensure that the hatch does not come adrift the first time someone carelessly stands on one side of the open lid. A combination of rubber seal and clamping bolts is common these days, but was not usual when this hatch was designed. No other arrangement is as reliable when it comes to excluding water from the inside of a yacht.

The rounded edges reduce the chances of ropes catching, look professional, and are easy to keep varnished or painted.

WATERTIGHT LOCKER

Wet gear makes for a miserable crew, and one way to keep things dry is to stow them in a locker which has been made watertight. The inside joins are cleaned, prepared, then glassed over using three runs of $1\frac{1}{2}$ ounce fibreglass cloth and plenty of resin.

The door must be strong, rigid and watertight, with a wide semi-soft rubber seal glued to its back. This seal needs proper mitred corners and ample glue to hold it firmly all round. To allow the door to be forced tight on the locker front there must be flexible hinges which can be made of webbing with large plate washers over.

The door clips must press firmly against the door front, and they may be those anti-rattle door fasteners sold by Simpson Lawrence (their catalogue number 1923000) through chandlers all over the world. They are like strong turn-buttons and are easy to use in bad weather when the boat is jumping about.

ENLARGED DETAIL

TURN-BUTTON SWINGS EITHER WAY AND PRESSES DOOR TIGHT SHUT

EDGE OF L'KER DOOR

WOOD CHOCK SAME THICKN͜S AS L'KER DOOR

ANTI-RATTLE DOOR FASTENER SPRING-LOADED

EDGE OF L'KER FRONT

SECTION THRU' LOCKER

FLEXIBLE HINGES

FOUR FASTENERS

FRONT of LOCKER DOOR

RIGID LOCKER DOOR FRAME WITH GLUED JOINTS

SEMI-SOFT RUBBER SEAL CONTINUOUS ALL ROUND

LOCKER FRONT FREE FROM DISTORTION

LOCKER MADE WATER-TIGHT BY FIBREGLASS TAPE

ENLARGED DETAIL

ENLARGED DETAIL at **X**

- METAL FLAT BAR WITH BOLTS THROUGH NEOPRENE AND COCKPIT WELL SIDE
- DRAIN HOLE FROM COCKPIT LOCKER
- NEOPRENE ⅛ INCH ~ 3ᴹ THICK FORMS VALVE

COCKPIT SOLE

BULKHEAD GLASSED FULLY ALL ROUND

LOCKER LID

CENTRE-LINE

JOIN IN BULKHᴰ FULLY GLASSED OVER

COCKPIT WELL

SEE DETAIL **X**

BULKHEAD EXTENDS WELL BELOW LOCKER BOTTOM FOR STRENGTH

FIDDLE KEEPS GEAR IN PLACE EVEN WHEN BOAT HEELS

- BULKHEAD OF PLYWOOD
- FOUR RUNS OF GLASSING
- LOCKER BASE OF 12MM ~ ½ INCH MARINE PLY
- STIFFENERS FORE-AND-AFT AND ATHWARTSHIPS AND DOWNWARDS
- LEDGE PIECE

ENLARGED DETAIL at **Y-Y**

MAKING A COCKPIT LOCKER WATERTIGHT

Water gets into a boat via cockpit lockers unless they are designed to be watertight and drain overboard or into the cockpit well. To seal off a cockpit locker, end bulkheads of ply, probably ½in (12mm) and certainly marine grade, are fitted. Where the shape is awkward, the top part will probably be fitted first, then the lower part which should extend well down. In the sketch, the bottom section goes right under the cockpit and so stiffens the well. When these two parts, A and B, have been fitted the locker bottom is fitted, parts C then D. The outboard part is tilted to encourage drainage and prevent the locker being too big and therefore a danger to the vessel in the event of flooding of the cockpit.

As the crew will sometimes want to climb into the locker, and there may at other times be a weight of water in it, the bottom needs proper reinforcing, as shown bottom left. Parts C and D are glassed together and glassed all round the edge. The bolts for many boats will be about ³⁄₈in (8mm) diameter, spaced typically about 8in (200mm).

A simple pair of valves, made from Neoprene sheeting, ensures that water drains out of the locker but does not trickle in from the cockpit well. (Detail top left.)

All this may seem a lot of work to prevent water getting inside the hull, and it is. But offshore sailors agree it is worth it. The alternative is to seal the cockpit locker lid and loose on-deck stowage. Some people prefer this approach.

COCKPIT STOWAGE

Underneath cockpit seats there are fine large lockers. Their big capacity is so useful for storing fenders, sailbags and other bulky things, but it is a disadvantage when it comes to finding a home for a couple of sheet winch handles, or small lengths of rope, sail tiers, spare shackles and such-like.

A sailmaker will stitch up panniers to any given size. He may use heavy gauge sail cloth or PVC or one of the man-made modern substitutes for traditional canvas. If there are several pouches in one locker it is a good idea to have them of different colours, then a stranger on board can be told that flares are in the red pouch, spinnaker sheets in the white one, and biscuits for the crew on watch in the blue one.

It may be advisable to have drain holes at the bottom of each pouch and these should be at least $1/2$in (12mm) diameter to prevent dirt clogging them. Get the sailmaker to use zig-zag stitching for ample strength along all the seams.

FOR ACCESS BELOW THE COCKPIT

Some cockpit wells have hatches in them, and these often leak. Some cockpits need new hatches through to the bottom, perhaps to reach a stern gland, or get a new tank in, or an old tank out. The hatch in the bottom of the well needs to be strong and properly sealed. This sketch shows a double seal for good measure, and an arrangement which can be used on a newly made or existing hatch.

Plywood, metal or fibreglass can be used for the hatch top. The holes for the vertical bolts round the hatch top are drilled under-size with the hatch lid positioned exactly, then the lid is taken off, and the holes in the angle-bar carefully threaded.

COCKPIT WELL SIDE OR END

DRAIN-WAY NO MORE THAN 1¼ INCHES ~30 MM WIDE TO AVOID CATCHING FEET

SEMI-PORTABLE HATCH IN COCKPIT SOLE

BRONZE OR STAINLESS STEEL COUNTER-SUNK BOLTS AT 4 INCH ~100 MM CENTRES

INNER SEMI-SOFT SEAL

Ian Nicolson

SOLE STIFFENER WITH TAPERED ENDS

THREADED HOLE FOR BOLT

SEMI-PORTABLE HATCH KEPT CLEAR OF DRAINS

CONTINUOUS OUTER SEMI-SOFT SEAL

ANGLE-BAR OF SAME MATERIAL AS BOLTS

COAMING PIECES WELL BEDDED DOWN

SECTION THROUGH COCKPIT BOTTOM HATCH

Boom Gallows

GOAL POST GALLOWS

The basis of this boom gallows is a single length of steel or aluminium tube bent into the shape of a goal with stiffening brackets at each top corner. In practice, there may be a forward or aft reaching diagonal leg each side, to give the gallows stability in the fore-and-aft plane. These support struts which are not shown in the drawing can be quite short, and may be of the same thin bar or tube used to strengthen the corners.

The chock which supports the boom hangs upside down when not in use. When the boom is to be lodged in the gallows, the crew can locate the chock anywhere along the top length of piping. The two locking handles are turned tightly to secure the chock, and the boom dropped in place. When the chock is hanging below the pipe, the boom with sail set just clears the top of the whole affair.

This type of gallows makes a marvellous grab-rail, and it can support a canvas dodger across the aft end of the cockpit, to make it snugger and safer.

ENLARGED DETAIL AT A-A

HARD-WOOD CHOCK SAME THICKNESS AS PIPE DIAMETER

METAL PLATE BENT ROUND TUBE. PLATE 1/8 INCH~3M THICK PER 20 FT.~6METRES OF BOAT LENGTH

STAGGERED SCREWS THROUGH PLATE

TWO NUTS WELDED TO PLATE

TWO LOCKING HANDLES

BOOM REST IN "ON MOORINGS" POSITION

SAIL SET

BOOM IN "WORKING" POSITION CLEAR OF GALLOWS

BOOM REST STOWED WHEN SAILING

PIPE FRAMEWORK 1INCH~25M DIAMETER PER 20 FT.~6METRES OF BOAT LENGTH

SIDE LEGS TILTED IN FOR STRENGTH & GOOD APPEARANCE

VIEW LOOKING FORWARD or AFT

HARD-WOOD BOOM REST

LEATHER SCALLOPED TO FIT ROUND CURVE

COUNTERSUNK HOLE FOR BOOM LASHING

<u>ENLARGED</u> <u>DETAILS</u>

Ian Nicolson

ROD STIFFENER

BENT TUBE FORMS BOOM GALLOWS

DROP-NOSE PINS

SAFETY LINE

REMOVE TOP OR BOTTOM PINS EACH SIDE TO FOLD GALLOWS FORW⁰ OR AFT

SIDE PLATE

BASE PLATE

STAINL^S STEEL OR GALVANISED PARTS

<u>FRONT OR</u> <u>BACK VIEW</u>

SAME BOTH SIDES

<u>SIDE VIEW</u>

WOOD CHOCKS UNDER BASE-PLATE MAY BE BEVELLED TO DEAL WITH DECK CAMBER

FOLDING BOOM GALLOWS

This simple gallows can be made to fold forward or aft, and by withdrawing both drop-nose pins each side, the whole fitting can be taken off the boat for storage or repairs.

Each base plate is secured to the deck or cabin top with four bolts. The height and width of the gallows is measured on the ship, and the tubular part is quickly made by anyone with a pipe-bending rig. The tube diameter would be about 1in (25mm) diameter for each 20ft (6m) of boat length. The diagonal stiffeners may not be essential, but they may prevent the gallows from being damaged by a careless gybe, if the mainsheet snags the gallows. The rod stiffeners will typically be one fifth of the tube diameter, or may be of tube one third the main tube diameter.

The top left sketch shows how the leather padding, designed to prevent the boom being damaged, is cut in scallops round the edge so that it will bend into a boom recess. Top right shows the metal plate welded to the top of the tube, to take the wooden boom rest.

VERTICAL SLIDING BOOM GALLOWS

This device used to be common on every sort of yacht, but is now seen mainly on large ones. However, it does make life aboard more comfortable on many occasions. It forms a marvellous support if a boom tent is rigged; it can help when reefing because the aft end of the boom can be lashed into the gallows; it is ideal when the mainsail is lowered in severe weather; and it forms a great grab-rail. Of course, its main use is for when the boat is on moorings.

The one shown is based on the *Myth of Malham* type which drops into the deck when out of use. Alternative details are shown. For instance, one side has a weight to keep the diagonal cross-wire tight, the other a length of thick shockcord. One side has a raised bearing for the support tube, the other a sunken one. One side has a strong plate bracket at the top of the tube, the other a lighter, more elegant but thinner bar bracket. Owners can choose which style they favour for these parts.

Some people do not cut a central slot for the boom, since they feel one port and one starboard are adequate. Just a few owners use brass or bronze for all the metal parts and keep them polished which looks superb.

ENLARGED DETAIL AT 'A-A'   SECTION VIEW

COUNTER-SUNK HOLES FOR BOOM LASHINGS
HARD-WOOD GALLOWS USUALLY VARNISHED
THROUGH CLENCHES OR BOLTS ZIG-ZAGGED
METAL PLATES AT SOCKETS

ROD BRACKET AND LASHING
TUBULAR METAL SUPPORTS
BUSHED HOLES IN DECK
RIGGING SCREW
PLATE BRACKET
FLEXIBLE WIRES
END STOP ON WIRE
DECK DOUBLER
WEIGHT DROPS WHEN GALLOWS ARE LOWERED
BELOW DECK BEARS TUBE
ABOVE DECK BEARING
SHOCK-CORD PULLS WIRE DOWN WHEN GALLOWS ARE LOWERED

Ian Nicolson

STITCHING

THICK LEATHER

OVAL BAR OR FLAT BAR
WITH EDGES GROUND OFF

ENLARGED SECTION
AT A-A

BOOM REST FITS BOOM SHAPE

EYES FOR BOOM
LASHING EACH SIDE

TUBE DIAMETER ¾ INCH ~ 20 ᴹᴹ
FOR EVERY 20 FEET ~ 6 METRES
OF BOAT'S LENGTH

RECESSED NUTS
WOOD CHOCKS
EACH SIDE

COAMING

WIDE METAL STRAP

UPSTANDING METAL PEG

FLANGE BOLTED DOWN

WOODEN CHOCK

COCKPIT SOLE OR SEAT

Ian Nicolson

Y-TYPE BOOM GALLOWS

This type of gallows is compact, easy to stow and to erect in harbour, and it does not take up much deck space. Against that, it is awkward to put up at sea, and not much good for holding the boom in very severe conditions offshore unless a pair of guys are fitted to give steadiness athwartships.

It is handy if the boom is used to support a cockpit tent or awning. The distance from the top to the metal strap should not be more than two and a half times the distance from the strap to the bottom. The bottom may be secured by another metal strap, or the upstanding peg shown here which fits firmly inside the end of the tube.

Traditionally, the top fork is padded with thick leather but as this material is expensive and not always easy to get, plastic pipe or PVC cloth may be used instead.

WOOD SINGLE-LEG BOOM GALLOWS

This type of gallows is cheap to make, easy to stow, and suits those people who have woodworking facilities but no metal-working tools. The usual padding in the mouth of the Y has been omitted in favour of the easily available and simple-to-fit lashing of thin rope.

The arms of the Y are glued and held by metal fastenings which, theoretically, are superfluous, and could be removed when the glue has set hard. Alternative fastening techniques are shown on the left and right sides. Long copper clenches are not much seen these days but they do look nautical, sensible and, to most people, decorative.

The strap round the middle could be made from metal, but the arrangement shown has the virtue that it is built up from the same material of the same thickness as the rest of the gallows. The bottom socket too can be glued up from layers of the same wood. It should have a drain hole quite $^5/\mathrm{s}$in (15mm) diameter to allow rain and spray to run away.

COUNTER-SUNK HOLES FOR BOOM LASHING

RENEW LASHING WHEN VARNISHING

NYLON LASHING ³⁄₁₆ INCH ~ 5 MM DIAMᵀᴿ PER 20 FT. ~ 6 METRES BOAT LENGTH FORMS PADDING

LARGE SCREWS OR COPPER CLENCHES [SHOWN RIGHT SIDE] OR BOLTS

BOOM LASHED IN PLACE

SINGLE-LEG GALLOWS

ENLARGE-MENT

GLUED JOINTS

HARDWOOD USUALLY VARNISHED

A   A

CLEARANCES TYPICALLY ¹⁄₁₆ INCH ~ 1 MM

DEEP SOCKET

COCKPIT SEAT

BOLTS WITH DOWELLED HEADS. BOLT DIAMᵀᴿ ³⁄₁₆ INCH ~ 5 MM PER 20 FT ~ 6 METRES OF BOAT LENGTH

LOOKᶢ FORWᴰ OR AFT

ENLARGED DETAIL ᴀᴛ A-A

TYPICAL OVERALL LENGTH BETW'N 10 & 16 FT. ~ 3 & 5 M'TRES

FORE-DECK STRENGTHENS BOAT AND KEEPS GEAR DRY

FOLDING HOOD KEEPS CREW AND GEAR DRY

"CAPTIVE" ROWLOCKS CANNOT BE LOST

SEATS WITH BUOYANCY UNDER

PORT & STARBOARD
STERN PAINTERS

Ian Nicholson

ADJUSTABLE FOOT-
REST FOR OARSMAN

SHELF OVER
BUOY'CY TANK

HULL SHAPE TO SUIT
ROWING OR OUTBOARD

U-BOLT FOR 25 FOOT
8 METRE ~ ⅜ INCH ~ 10 M
DIAM'TR BOW PAINTER

METAL-SHOD SKEG WITH HAND-HOLE

BILGE KEELS WITH BRASS RUBBING STRIPS
PROTECT HULL WHEN BEACHING

MOORINGS
TENDER

GETTING OUT TO THE YACHT

The usual yacht's tender, whether it is an inflatable or a solid dinghy, is far from ideal for getting the crew and their gear out to the parent yacht at the beginning of a weekeend. The popular type of tender is small so as to be easy to lift aboard and stow conveniently. It rows badly (especially if it is an inflatable), it does not carry much gear, sometimes not all the crew in one load, and it does not keep crew or their gear dry.

What so many people need is a larger rowing or outboard dinghy just for getting to and from the home moorings. It can be an old boat and it need not be light provided there are good facilities for launching it. Alternatively, it can be kept afloat all the time, possibly on a running line secured to the shore.

It does need to have ample freeboard, but if it is narrow it will be easier to row. It should be as large as possible and must support everyone on board with 6in (150mm) of freeboard if flooded. It must be able to stand up to beaching, and have lots of fendering all round. Bow and stern painters are essential for tying alongside the parent yacht.

A MORE COMFORTABLE INFLATABLE DINGHY

Many inflatable dinghies have rowing thwarts which are inflatable, but such seats do not make for easy rowing. Those dinghies which have solid seats often have them set on top of the inflated side tubes, and this is too high for rowing. The top sketch shows how a rigid seat of the correct height is easily made.

Almost as important, there should be a 'stretcher' or footrest for the oarsman. Since people are not all the same height, the footrest should be adjustable fore and aft. The bottom sketch is an enlargement of the bottom boards and footrest, as well as the footrest support.

If an inflatable dinghy has no solid bottom boards it will be hard to row. As marine ply is expensive and heavy, the bottom boards shown here are made up of a relatively thin sheet of ply with stiffeners top and bottom. The top ones act as toe rails and prevent the crew slipping, the bottom ones reduce local chafe caused by the bottom boards.

SECTION AT B-B
ENLARGED DETAIL

BOX SECTION SEAT OF THIN PLY

LAMINATED OR "GROWN" KNEE. TWO EACH SIDE

PADDING

FRONT, BACK, & END FILLER PIECES 2½×1 INCH ~ 60×25 MM

DINGHY BOTTOM

SIDE TUBE OF INFLATABLE DINGHY

EXTRA HIGH WATER-PROOF HOOD

PLASTIC OR METAL SUPPORT HOOPS

SOLID SEAT FOR OARSMAN

Ian Nicolson

VARIABLE FOOT-REST

PINE FOOT REST 2 INCHES ~ 50 MM DEEP & 1½ INCHES ~ 40 MM THICK

HARDWOOD 1 INCH ~ 25 MM THICK

¾ INCH ~ 20 MM DRAIN-HOLES

⅜ INCH ~ 10 MM MARINE PLY

1×½ INCH ~ 25×12 MM HALF-ROUNDS GLUED ON AT 6 INCH ~ 150 MM CENTRES

SECTION AT A-A
ENLARGED DETAIL

2×2 INCH~50×50 MM WOOD BAR

VIEW AT
ARROW 'A'
ENLARGED

SIDE
PIECE

BASE PIECE IS FULL WIDTH
ACROSS INSIDE OF DINGHY

HIGH SPEED ELECTRIC AIR
PUMP FOR QUICK INFLATION

SHORT ELECTRIC LEADS TO PORTABLE BATTERY
OR LONG LEADS TO BOAT'S MAIN BATTERY

LINE EACH SIDE ROUND
ROWLOCK HOLDS FOOT-REST

A

Ian Nicolson

FOOT-REST FOR OARSMAN.
SEE ENLARGED DETAIL

POUCH GLUED IN TO HOLD BOTTLE

DOUBLING PATCH GLUED ON AREA
WHICH SUFFERS FROM CHAFE

PAINTER OF ROPE WHICH FLOATS WILL NOT FOUL PROPELLER

EYESPLICE IN PAINTER END JUST FITS OVER YACHT'S STERN CLEAT

IMPROVING AN INFLATABLE

Most inflatables are hard to row, not least because they have no stretcher, or footrest for the oarsman. It is difficult to fix a footrest in an inflatable which has no bottom boards, so the design shown here, or a similar one, has to be used.

Wear on the bottom, especially aft, is the main reason why many inflatables leak and chafe to destruction. This trouble can be eliminated by doubling the bottom with a piece of canvas, tough rubberised cloth or a similar resilient material.

Even their best friends admit that it is a slow tedious job blowing up an inflatable. Also it can be frustrating trying to get the air out when the time comes to stow the dinghy in a small locker. A 12-volt air pump is now popular for inflating and deflating, both in emergencies and for everyday use.

Index